W9-BRI-117

# ALASKA Roadhouse Recipes

Memorable recipes from roadhouses, lodges,
bed and breakfasts, cafés, restaurants and campgrounds
along the highways and byways of Alaska and Canada

From the Editors of The MILEPOST®

**Photography:** All photos courtesy of the recipe contributors, with the exception of those listed below.
Jerrianne Lowther, pages 55, 107, 113, 118, 129, 171, 181, 207, 214; Earl L. Brown, pages 20, 27, 51, 82, 103, 116, 194; Sharon Nault, pages 4, 7, 59, 65, 91; Judy Parkin, page 198. Mary Carey photo on page 60 courtesy of "The Frontiersman/Valley Sun."

**Cover Photo:** Chef Greybeard of Alaska Wildland Adventures shows off his Skilak Omelet. (Photo courtesy of Alaska Wildland Adventures)

Recipes were solicited from the contributors. Recipes were reviewed by editors and in some cases tested, but the publisher offers no guarantee of individual results.

**Design:** David L. Ranta
**Editor:** Kris Valencia

## ALASKA Roadhouse Recipes

Published by
**The MILEPOST®**
301 Arctic Slope Ave., Suite 300
Anchorage, AK 99518
www.themilepost.com

Design, Typography, and Production
**The MILEPOST®**
Anchorage, Alaska

Printing
**Branch Smith**
Fort Worth, Texas

©1997 MCC Magazines, LLC. All rights reserved.

Manufactured in the United States of America

This book is protected by copyright law. No material may be copied, faxed, electronically transmitted, reproduced, or otherwise used without express written permission. Requests must be submitted in writing to The MILEPOST®.

Second Printing: 2007

ISBN 9-781892-15425

# CONTENTS

P hoto of the old Sourdough Roadhouse, located at Mile 147.5 Richardson Highway, was taken in the early 1980s. The historic structure offered gas, food and lodging to highway travelers until it burned down in December 1992.

# INTRODUCTION

oadhouse. In the North, this term refers to those early-day hostelries along the trails used by dog-team, horse-drawn sled and wagon stage. Spaced about a day's journey apart (by horse or by dog), the roadhouse offered food and shelter to everyone from miners to missionaries.

Today, roadhouse means the same as lodge, hotel, bed and breakfast, or campground. It is an outpost of hospitality in a very large land. The modern-day equivalents of those early-day roadhouses offer that same Northern hospitality: a place to stay and a good meal for their guests. Many of these modern-day hosts have generously shared their recipes with us, from the hotel chef's haute cuisine to the roadhouse cook's more basic grub.

Of the hundreds of roadhouses in the early days of the North, relatively few remain. Many have simply vanished, while the ruins of others may be seen along the road. These include the old Black Rapids Lodge, described as the "farthest north of the old-time Richardson trail hostelries," which is still visible along the Richardson Highway. The Central Roadhouse site, on the National Register of Historic Places, may be seen from the Steese Highway near Central, Alaska.

A few roadhouses became private homes. Others housed different businesses over the years, more often than not a bar. Fire has claimed many old structures, such as the Sourdough Roadhouse and the Richardson Roadhouse. The Blix Roadhouse in Copper Center, Alaska, which operated during the gold rush days of 1897-1898, was destroyed by fire, but was replaced by the Copper Center Lodge in 1932.

Other roadhouses and lodges—Paxson, Manley, Talkeetna, Gakona, Eureka, Sheep Mountain, Tiekel River and Tsaina, to name a few—have survived, and continue to offer travelers a warm bed and a hot meal on a cold night. These survivors have been renovated, and sometimes completely rebuilt, but they retain the spirit of the original roadhouse.

Diana Graf of Rika's Roadhouse, which is now part of a state historical park, writes: "Roadhouses smelled of fireplace wood and moose hide. Pioneers and visitors swapped stories in warm parlors, where there were big, creaking rocking chairs and tables littered with long-out-of-date magazines. Meals were served at long tables covered with oil cloth and there were beaten paths outside leading to the outhouses."

Indoor plumbing has pretty much replaced the outhouses, but the shared warmth of the fire, the shared meal and the shared stories among travelers can still be found among the hostelries of the North.

This collection of recipes salutes the hosts of the North and their businesses, whether they date back a century or a decade; whether they are roadhouses, bed and breakfasts or campgrounds; whether they are found along the historic Richardson Highway in Alaska, the Klondike Highway in Yukon, or the Yellowhead Highway in British Columbia. Eat and enjoy!

# Breakfasts

**E**stablished in 1903, the Sourdough Roadhouse was approved as a historical site by the state of Alaska in the spring of 1974 and became a national historic landmark in 1979. It was the oldest roadhouse in Alaska still operating in the original building until it burned down in December 1992. The roadhouse was located at Mile 147.5 Richardson Highway. When it was still in business, the Sourdough Roadhouse advertised "family atmosphere, good home-cooked food" and a "sourdough breakfast anytime." Some outbuildings remain, and nearby a portion of the old Valdez trail is still visible. Used by gold stampeders to the Klondike in 1898, the Valdez trail led from the port of Valdez to Eagle. It was later converted to a wagon road and eventually became today's Richardson Highway.

# ALMOST FAMOUS GRANOLA

*Wenda Lythgoe & Brent Liddle, The Cabin Bed & Breakfast*
*Km 219 Haines Highway*

"You can leave out or add in any other suitable granola ingredients to your liking. You can also increase or decrease any of the ingredients. Make it your own!"

5 cups **old-fashioned oats**
5 cups **regular oats**
1 cup **raw bran**
1/2 to 1 cup **oat bran and/or wheat germ**
1/2 to 3/4 cup **brown sugar**
1 cup **sunflower seeds**
1 cup **sesame seeds**
1 cup **pumpkin seeds**
2 Tb. **flax seeds**
1/2 cup **skim-milk powder**
2 cups **chopped nuts (I use sliced almonds and pecans)**
1 cup **unsweetened ribbon coconut**
1/2 cup **frozen orange juice or apple juice concentrate**
1/2 cup **water**
1/2 cup **vegetable oil**
1/2 to 1 cup **honey**
1 Tb. **vanilla**
1 to 2 tsp. (or to taste) **cinnamon, nutmeg OR ginger, optional**
1 cup **dried fruit**

tart with the oats in a large mixing bowl. Add next 10 ingredients. In a saucepan, combine juice, water, oil, honey, vanilla and optional spices. Heat gently to melt honey and mix ingredients. Pour slowly over granola and mix well to coat evenly. Put in  9" x 13" baking pans or larger size, approximately 1 inch deep. Bake, uncovered, at 325°F for 30 minutes or until lightly browned. Stir every 5 to 10 minutes, and more frequently towards the end of baking, to prevent the granola on the edges of pan from burning. Remove from oven.

Add 1 cup chopped, dried fruit (raisins, apples, apricots, peaches, etc.) and let cool, stirring occasionally. Store in an airtight container in a cool place, or it keeps in the freezer for months. Makes approximately 20 cups.

# GOOD MORNING GRANOLA

*Jon and Nelda Osgood*
*Tutka Bay Wilderness Lodge, Homer*

6 cups **rolled oats**
1 cup **wheat germ, untoasted**
1 cup **sesame seeds**
1 cup **sunflower seeds**
1 cup **shredded coconut**
1 cup **sliced almonds**
1 cup **dried fruit (raisins, cranberries, dates, apricots, etc.)**
1 cup **nonfat dry milk**
1 cup **oil**
1 cup **honey**

Preheat the oven to 300°F. In a large bowl, combine all of the dry ingredients. Drizzle the oil and honey over the dry ingredients and mix very well. Spread the mixture on a large baking sheet, and toast in the oven for 30 to 40 minutes, stirring every 10 minutes. Remove mixture from the oven when it is lightly browned. If it gets too brown, it will taste burned. Cool completely and store refrigerated in an airtight container. Granola will keep for several weeks. Makes 15 cups, or enough for 30 1/2-cup servings.

# HELGA'S HOT CEREAL

*Helga Garrison, Helga's B&B, Sitka*

"The dish needs to be prepared the night before, or it won't taste right."

1 1/2 cups of milk (or more if needed)
2 cups cooked, firm rice (do not use instant rice)
1 cup diced, dry apricots
2 unpeeled apples, diced
1 cup raisins
1 tsp. cinnamon
1/2 tsp. cloves
2 eggs

The night before, mix all of the ingredients together in a large bowl. It will be very thin. Put in a 9" x 13" baking pan (that is sprayed with nonstick spray). In the morning, dot with butter, if you wish. Bake at 375°F for 45 minutes. Serve plain or with toast. Can also be eaten cold as a snack later in the day. Serves 8.

# BAKED APPLE PANCAKE

*Sharon Waisanen, Spruce Avenue Bed & Breakfast
Soldotna*

"The Finnish name for this pancake is 'Omenapannukakku.' Our son, Kyle, has requested this pancake for years as his favorite. Our guests love it, too."

| | |
|---|---|
| 4 eggs | 3 large apples, peeled, |
| 1¹/₂ cups milk | cored and sliced |
| ¹/₂ tsp. salt | cinnamon sugar (¹/₂ cup sugar and |
| 2 Tb. sugar mixed with | 3 tsp. cinnamon) |
| 2 cups sifted white flour | whipped cream (or whipped topping) |

Beat eggs well; add milk, salt and sugar. Sift in flour, mixing it well. Let the batter stand for 30 minutes. Butter well two 8- or 9-inch round cake pans (or a 9" x 13" rectangular pan), and sprinkle with part of the cinnamon sugar. Arrange the sliced apples in the pans. Sprinkle the apples with cinnamon sugar (save some of the sugar to sprinkle over the batter). Pour the pancake batter over the apples, dividing it evenly between the pans. Sprinkle with remaining cinnamon sugar.

Bake in a moderately hot oven (375°F) for about 30 minutes or until the top of pancake is golden and set. This is best served immediately, but can be reheated before serving. Serve plain or with cream (or whipped topping). We also serve it with rhubarb, lingonberry or raspberry jam. Serves 2 to 4.

# BANANA NUT PANCAKES

*Kim Kirby, Millar Street House Bed & Breakfast*
*Ketchikan*

"Guests at our B&B always enjoy these pancakes, which we serve when the skies are grey and Ketchikan is receiving just some of its 13 feet of rain. They seem to give the energy required to take on the day."

1¹/₂ cups **sifted all-purpose flour**
1 tsp. **salt**
3 Tb. **sugar**
1³/₄ tsp. **baking powder**
1 **slightly beaten egg**
3 Tb. **melted butter**
1 to 1¹/₄ cups **milk**
1 **mashed banana**
¹/₂ cup **chopped pecans**

Sift together flour, salt, sugar and baking powder. In a separate bowl, combine egg, butter, milk, banana and pecans. Mix the liquid ingredients with the dry ingredients swiftly and let rest for 10 minutes. Cook by spooning mixture onto a hot griddle for about 2 to 3 minutes on each side. Serve with hot maple syrup and butter. Serves 6.

# "DREAM" OVEN PANCAKE

*Sharon Waisanen, Spruce Avenue Bed & Breakfast*
*Soldotna*

"The Finnish name for this pancake is 'Unelemapannukakku.' We like topping this pancake with homemade blueberry jam, whipped cream and slices of kiwi fruit."

1 cup **whipping cream**
2 **eggs**
2 Tb. **sugar**
1/2 cup **sifted white flour**
1 1/2 Tb. **melted butter**

**W**hip the cream until stiff, and set aside. Beat together the eggs and sugar until very light. Fold in half of the whipped cream. Sift the flour over the cream/egg mixture, fold it in well, then fold in the melted butter. Pour into a well-buttered 8- or 9-inch flan pan (or round cake pan) and bake at 375°F for 15 minutes. Top with jam, the remaining whipped cream and fresh fruit slices before serving. Serves 2.

# FINNISH OVEN PANCAKE

*Sharon Waisanen, Spruce Avenue Bed & Breakfast*
*Soldotna*

4 **eggs**
2 Tb. **sugar**
2³/₄ cups **milk**
1 tsp. **salt**
1³/₄ cups **flour**

reheat oven to 425°F.
Beat eggs and sugar well. Add milk and salt. Gradually add flour, beating until thoroughly mixed. Butter a 9" x 13" pan. Pour in batter. Bake for 20 to 25 minutes. Serve with jam, syrup or fresh fruit, and/or whipped topping.

# GINGERBREAD PANCAKES WITH LEMON CURD

*Judy Urquhart, Blueberry Lodge Bed and Breakfast*
*Juneau*

"This is the most requested recipe at Blueberry Lodge B&B."

2¹/₂ cups **flour**
5 tsp. **baking powder**
1 tsp. **baking soda**
1¹/₂ tsp. **salt**
1 tsp. **cinnamon**
¹/₂ tsp. **ginger**
2 **eggs**
2 cups **milk**

¹/₄ cup **molasses**
1 cup **raisins**

**Lemon Curd:**
3 **eggs**
¹/₂ cup **sugar**
²/₃ cup **lemon juice**
6 Tb. **melted butter**
**zest of lemon (optional)**

In a large bowl, combine flour, baking powder, baking soda, salt, cinnamon and ginger. In a separate bowl, beat eggs slightly, then stir in milk and molasses. Pour egg mixture into dry ingredients. Stir only until moistened. Stir in raisins. Pour pancakes onto griddle. Flip when bubbles show through. Serve with syrup and lemon curd. Serves 5 to 6.

For lemon curd, combine eggs, sugar and lemon juice. Add melted butter and mix well. Microwave on low, stirring with whisk every 2 minutes, until thick. Stir in lemon zest. Serve warm on top of pancakes.

# OVERNIGHT SOURDOUGH PANCAKES

*Ked Schoming, Morning Glory B&B, Homer*

2 cups **warm water**
1 tsp. **yeast, at room temperature**
2 cups **flour**
1 tsp. **salt**
2 Tb. **sugar**
1 Tb. **oil**
1 **egg**
1 tsp. **baking soda**

The night before, mix yeast in warm water until dissolved. Mix flour and yeast together. Cover and let sit in a warm place overnight. (Important: Do not use a metal pan or spoon.)

The next morning, mix salt, sugar, oil, egg and baking soda with yeast and flour mixture to desired consistency (add water for thinner batter) and cook on a 350°F grill. Makes 18 medium-size pancakes.

# SAUSAGE OVEN PANCAKE

*Sharon Waisanen, Spruce Avenue Bed & Breakfast*
*Soldotna*

"The main recipes we use at our B&B are all Finnish oven pancakes. This is a Finnish recipe known as 'Makkarapannukakku.'"

**2 eggs**
**1¹/₂ cups milk**
**1¹/₂ cups white flour**
**1 tsp. baking powder**
**1 tsp. salt**
**¹/₂ lb. sausage (I use ham slices or reindeer sausage)**
**1 small onion, sliced**
**¹/₂ cup shredded cheddar cheese**

eat the eggs well. Add milk, flour, baking powder and salt. Butter a 9" x 13" pan well. Arrange slices of sausage and onions in layers. Pour pancake batter over, then sprinkle the cheese evenly over the batter. Bake at 400°F for about 20 minutes or until golden brown. Serve with jam, syrup, fresh fruit or whipped topping. Serves 2 to 4.

# SWEDISH OVEN PANCAKE

*Camp Denali and North Face Lodge*
*Denali National Park*

"Resembling a large popover, this breakfast dish is impressive when served at the table from a cast iron skillet. It must come directly from the oven, as it will gradually fall. We recommend a topping of lingonberry sauce and yogurt. Commercial whole cranberry sauce may be substituted for lingonberries."

| | |
|---|---|
| 3 strips **bacon** | 1 cup **flour** |
| 3 **eggs** | 2 Tb. **sugar** |
| 2 cups **milk** | 1/2 tsp. **salt** |

**C**ut bacon up and brown it until crisp in a 12- or 13-inch-diameter frying pan.* Do not pour off drippings. Beat eggs and milk together lightly, or combine in a blender. Add flour, sugar and salt, and blend together only until ingredients are combined. Do not overmix. Reheat pan with bacon drippings, and then pour in batter. It should sizzle when added to the pan. Bake in a preheated 375°F oven until lightly browned and puffed (30 minutes). Bring to the table immediately, cut and serve with fruit or berry preserves, syrup or fresh-squeezed lemon juice and a dusting of powdered sugar. Serves 4 to 5.

*A smaller frying pan can be used, and the bacon and drippings transferred to the equivalent of a 9" x 13" baking pan. Reheat pan and drippings before adding batter.

# MOOSE CREEK SOURDOUGH PANCAKES

*Don and Joanne Lefler, Moose Creek Lodge*
*Mile 229.1 Klondike Highway*

2²/₃ cups **flour**
4 Tb. **sugar**
2 Tb. **baking powder**
2 tsp. **salt**
2 **eggs**
1¹/₄ cups **milk**
1¹/₄ cups **sourdough starter**
  (see recipe following)
1¹/₄ cups **water**
6 Tb. **oil**
¹/₂ tsp. **vanilla**

Combine flour, sugar, baking powder and salt, and set aside. In separate bowl, combine eggs, milk, starter, water, oil and vanilla, and mix thoroughly. Add dry ingredients. Cook by spooning mixture onto a hot griddle for about 2 to 3 minutes on each side. Serves 6 to 8.

## Sourdough Starter

1 cup **flour**
1 cup **warm water**
1 package **active dry yeast**
1 Tb. **sugar**

ix the ingredients thoroughly in a gallon jar (to allow room to triple). Let mix stand, loosely covered, for a day or two, until it is frothy and full of bubbles. The bubbling will begin shortly after you mix the ingredients, but it will take a longer time for the bubbles to permeate the mixture and for the sour smell of sourdough to develop.

After mixture has fermented and soured, stir it down and refrigerate. It will be better after it has aged a few days in the refrigerator. Replenish after each use.

To replenish starter, replace equal amounts of flour and water according to amount of starter used (for example, if you use 1 cup of starter, replace with 1 cup of flour and 1 cup of water), stir and return to fridge.

# TREEHOUSE SIGNATURE SOURDOUGH PANCAKES

*Jessie Marrs, Alaska's Treehouse Bed & Breakfast, Seward*

The sourdough starter used in this pancake recipe needs to sit for 5 days. Serve these pancakes with Lowbush Cranberry Butter (see recipe under Sauces, Syrups & Preserves).

2¹/₂ cups **flour**

2 cups **warm water**

1 cup **sourdough starter (see recipe following)**

¹/₄ cup **powdered skim milk**

1 **egg**

2 Tb. **sugar**

1 tsp. **salt**

1 tsp. **baking soda**

The night before mix flour with the warm water and add starter. Stir well and cover with a damp cloth. In the morning, take out 1 cup of starter and reserve for future use (store in refrigerator). Add powdered milk and egg to remaining batter, beating well. Combine sugar, salt and baking soda; sprinkle evenly over batter, then fold in gently. Let batter rest a few minutes. Cook on a hot, oiled griddle. Serves 4.

## Sourdough Starter

1 Tb. dry yeast
2¹/₂ cups warm water
2 tsp. sugar OR honey
2¹/₂ cups flour

ix together ingredients and let ferment 5 days at room temperature, stirring daily. Starter will keep indefinitely in the refrigerator, but should be used once a week.

# BAKED PEACH FRENCH TOAST

*James G. Beard, Arctic Fox Inn, Anchorage*

1 large loaf **unsliced French bread**
8 **eggs, well beaten**
6 cups **whole or 2% milk**
¹/₂ cup **brown sugar**
1 Tb. vanilla
1 large can **sliced peaches**
2 cups **whipping cream**
1 **whole fresh nutmeg, grated just before serving**

**S**lice French bread into thick slices and leave unwrapped overnight to harden. Beat eggs and milk with sugar and vanilla. Soak bread slices thoroughly and grill over medium heat until lightly crusty. Place overlapping in baking dishes and surround with peach slices. Bake at 350°F for 30 minutes. Whip cream while French toast is baking. Decorate edge of pan with whipped cream and grate fresh nutmeg over all. Serve immediately. Serves 12.

# FOTZELSCHNITTEN (SWISS FRENCH TOAST)

*Brigitte Suter*
*Brigitte's Bavarian Bed & Breakfast, Homer*

1/4 cup **milk**
4 **eggs**
**salt**
**nutmeg**
8 stale slices **brown bread**
3 Tb. **butter**
**plum jam, applesauce OR maple syrup**

eat the milk in a small saucepan, until warm. Beat the eggs, adding salt and nutmeg to taste in a separate bowl. Stick the bread slices on a fork, and dip first in the milk and then in the eggs. Melt a part of the butter in a fry pan. Add 2 to 3 slices of bread and fry until golden brown on both sides. Put in warm place and proceed in the same way with the rest of the bread. Serve with plum jam, applesauce or maple syrup. Serves 4.

# FREEZER FRENCH TOAST

*Lolita Valcq, Rock Creek Bed & Breakfast*
*Mile 261 George Parks Highway*

"This is a favorite with my bed-and-breakfast guests. I can cater to large groups, so this is great to do the night before."

4 **eggs**
1 cup **milk**
1 Tb. **sugar**
1 tsp. **vanilla**
$1/4$ tsp. **nutmeg**
$1/4$ tsp. **cinnamon**
8 slices **French bread, $3/4$- to 1-inch thick**
**melted butter**

In a medium-size bowl, beat together the eggs, milk, sugar, vanilla, nutmeg and cinnamon. Place bread slices on a rimmed baking sheet. Pour egg mixture over all until the egg mixture is absorbed. Freeze, uncovered, until firm. Package in freezer bags and return to freezer until ready to use. To serve, place desired number of frozen slices on a lightly greased baking sheet. Brush each slice with melted butter and bake in a 400°F oven for 8 minutes. Turn slices over, brush with melted butter, and bake an additional 10 minutes or until nicely browned. Serve topped with powdered sugar, honey or syrup. Serves 4.

# SCOTCH TOAST

*Gail M. LaRocque, Cinnamon Cache Bakery & Coffee Shop, Mile 72 Klondike Highway South*

**2 eggs**
**¹/₂ cup milk**
**¹/₄ tsp. cinnamon**
**4 to 6 slices raisin bread**
**1 to 2 cups quick-cooking rolled oats**

**B**eat eggs, milk and cinnamon together. Dip bread into egg mixture then dredge through rolled oats. Fry until golden brown. Serve with favorite syrup. Serves 2 to 3.

# SKILAK OMELET

*Chef Greybeard, Alaska Wildland Adventures*
*Mile 50.1 Sterling Highway*

1 1/2 cups **fresh, sliced mushrooms**
1/3 cup **chopped onion**
1 1/2 cups **fresh asparagus, cut into 1-inch pieces**
9 **eggs**
1/4 cup **milk**
1/8 tsp. **pepper**
1/3 tsp. **garlic salt**
1 Tb. **chopped fresh parsley (or** 1 tsp. **dried)**
1 Tb. **butter or margarine**
3/4 cup **mozzarella, shredded**
1/4 cup **cheddar cheese, shredded**

Preheat oven to 325°F. Sauté mushrooms and onion. Set aside and keep warm. Boil or steam the asparagus until hot but still crisp, 2 to 3 minutes. Do not overcook. Set aside and keep warm.

Combine eggs, milk, pepper, garlic salt and parsley, and whip well. Melt butter in an oven-proof, 10-inch nonstick frying pan until melted and beginning to bubble. Pour in egg mixture and cook for 2 to 3 minutes until edges begin to firm. Insert a spatula into the mixture so you can lift the middle of the cooked egg allowing the uncooked to flow under the middle of the omelet.

Cook for 1 minute and lift center again. Begin lifting the edges by sliding a spatula gently under the edges and lifting as you tilt the pan to permit the remaining uncooked egg to flow under the edges into the bottom of the pan. Continue to do this all around the edge, building up the omelet as evenly as possible until the eggs no longer flow. Place the pan on the top rack of the preheated oven for 3 to 4 minutes or until the top of the omelet is cooked but not browned. Remove pan and turn off oven.

Spoon sautéed mushrooms and onions over eggs. Add asparagus. Sprinkle with mozzarella and top with cheddar. Place the pan back in the oven for 2 to 3 minutes to allow cheeses to set.

Using a spatula, loosen the omelet completely, then slide the spatula under the omelet opposite the handle and, as you tip the pan, lift and slide the omelet onto your serving dish. Clean the edges of overcooked egg/cheese. Cut into pie-shaped wedges by chopping downward with the end of a metal spatula. Do not try to slice across omelet or the cheese will stick and pull away. Serves 6.

"Greybeard" is an Alaskan Bush resident, who works as morning chef for Alaska Wildland Adventures Kenai River trips. (Alaska Wildland Adventures operates backcountry lodges on the Kenai and in Denali Park.) He spends his winter months on Caribou Island, Skilak Lake, gathering his winter supply of wood, snowmachining, cross-country skiing, painting with acrylics and dreaming up new recipes.

# ALASKAN SOURDOUGH SMOKED YUKON KING SALMON OMELET

*Willie and Lovie Johnson*
*Alaskan Sourdough Bed and Breakfast, Cooper Landing*

1/2 cup **chopped onion**
1/2 cup **sliced celery**
1/2 cup **diced green pepper**
1/2 cup **sliced mushrooms**
3 cups **smoked Yukon king salmon, shredded**
**salt, pepper and Cajun spices to taste**
16 **eggs, lightly whipped**

auté onion, celery, green pepper and mushrooms in a large fry pan. Add 1/2 cup of the salmon, and salt, pepper and Cajun spices. Add eggs and cook until almost done. Fold in remainder of salmon and cook for about 2 additional minutes. Serves 8.

# EASY GARDEN QUICHE

*Theresa Ely, Birch Grove Inn Bed and Breakfast*
*Fairbanks*

1 cup **shredded Swiss cheese**
1 cup **shredded cheddar cheese**
1¹/₂ cups **chopped vegetables (red peppers, mushrooms,**
  **yellow summer squash, zucchini)**
¹/₂ cup **milk**
¹/₂ cup **whipping cream**
6 **eggs**
¹/₄ tsp. **salt**
¹/₄ tsp. **nutmeg**
¹/₈ tsp. **pepper**

**H**eat oven to 375°F. Spray 10-inch quiche pan with nonstick spray. Sprinkle cheeses on bottom of prepared pan. Add chopped vegetables. In large bowl, whisk together milk, cream, eggs, salt, nutmeg and pepper. Pour egg mixture over vegetables. Bake for 40 to 45 minutes or until just set in the center. Serves 6.

# EASY SPINACH QUICHE

*Helen Tucker, Bed & Breakfast On The Park, Anchorage*

1 lb. cooked potatoes
olive oil
2 tsp. seasoning salt
8 eggs
2 cups milk
1 package frozen chopped spinach, thawed
1 cup shredded cheddar cheese
1/4 cup parmesan cheese

Slice cooked potatoes into 1/4-inch pieces, and lightly toss with olive oil and 1 tsp. seasoning salt, then place on bottom and sides of quiche pan. Mix eggs, milk and remaining salt together. Squeeze thawed spinach dry and add to eggs. Stir in cheeses and pour mixture over potatoes. Bake for 20 mintes at 375°F, then turn down oven to 350°F and bake until knife inserted in the center comes out clean. Serve warm or at room temperature. Serves 8.

# FIREWEED QUICHE

*Jeff Watts, Fireweed House Bed & Breakfast, Juneau*

6 oz. smoked salmon, skinned and flaked
pie crust
1 cup cooked wild rice
6 oz. grated Gruyere cheese
6 oz. grated Swiss cheese
2 cups cream
1 1/4 tsp. dry mustard
1/2 tsp. pepper
1/2 tsp. dill
3 eggs

L ayer salmon on top of unbaked crust, and add wild rice and cheeses. In a separate pan, heat cream, mustard, pepper and dill until scalded. Rapidly beat in eggs and pour into crust. Bake at 375°F for 35 minutes, or until center is no longer jiggly. Remove from oven and let set for a few minutes before cutting. Serves 6 to 8.

# SALMON QUICHE

*Jolene Schnell*
*At Schnell's Bed and Breakfast, Anchorage*

8 **eggs**
2 cups **cottage cheese**
2 tsp. **Dijon mustard**
pinch **of salt**
pinch **of pepper**
$1/2$ cup **finely chopped onion**
$3/4$ lb. **smoked salmon, flaked OR** $3/4$ to 1 lb. **fresh broiled salmon**
$1/2$ lb. **sautéed mushrooms (optional)**
**prepared pie shell**

Mix eggs, cottage cheese, mustard, salt, pepper and onion. Add salmon and mushrooms (if desired). Pour into pie shell. Bake at 350°F for 1 to 1$1/4$ hours. Serves 6 to 8.

# GABLES FRITTATA

*Leicha Welton, 7 Gables Inn, Fairbanks*

8 oz. **sausage**
2 cups **shredded zucchini**
2 **green onions, chopped**
$1/2$ tsp. **dry basil**
1 tsp. **Italian seasoning (dressing mix)**
6 **eggs**
$1/2$ cup **half and half OR whipping cream**
4 oz. **cream cheese, cut in cubes**
1 cup each **mozzarella and cheddar cheese, shredded**

Preheat oven to 325°F. Spray an 8-inch pie plate with non-stick cooking spray. Brown sausage, drain, and place in prepared pan. Spread zucchini and onions over sausage; sprinkle with seasonings. Beat eggs with half and half, and pour over vegetables and sausage. Sprinkle cubed cream cheese, mozarella and cheddar cheese over the top. Bake for 45 minutes or until the middle is set and top is lightly browned. Serves 6.

# BREAKFAST TURNOVERS

*Carol Kleckner, Birch Haven Inn Bed & Breakfast, Fairbanks*

"This is a great recipe to put together the night before. Bake in the morning and serve with fruit garnish and home-fried potatoes."

2 sheets (17-oz. package) **frozen puff pastry**
4 Tb. **finely chopped green onion**
2 Tb. **butter, melted**
2 **eggs, beaten**
2 cups **shredded Swiss cheese**
2 cups **ham, chopped (vegetarian substitute: mushrooms)**
2 tsp. **dill**
¹/₂ tsp. **garlic powder**
¹/₂ tsp. **pepper**

haw pastry sheet for approximately 30 minutes. Separate sheets and fold each into a 12-inch square. Cut into quarters for a total of 8 squares. In a mixing bowl, combine all other ingredients. Place ¹/₂-cup of filling in center of each square. Moisten pastry edges with a little water and fold in half, pressing all sides together with a fork. Place on baking sheets. Bake at 400°F for 20 to 25 minutes until golden brown. If prepared the night before, cover baking sheets and refrigerate overnight, then bake as directed in the morning. Serves 8.

# EASY EGG SOUFFLÉ
*LesLee Solberg, Denali View Bed & Breakfast*
*Mile 3.1 Talkeetna Spur Road*

**4 eggs**
1¹/₂ tsp. **salsa**
¹/₃ cup plus 2 heaping tsp. **grated cheddar cheese, divided**
³/₄ cup **buttermilk (or less, depending on the density of the eggs)**
1 Tb. **Bisquick**

Preheat oven to 350°F. Mix together eggs, salsa, ¹/₃ cup cheese, buttermilk and Bisquick. Spray custard cups or small, oven-proof bowls with nonstick cooking spray and pour mixture into bowls, to ³/₄-inch from the top of the bowl. Bake in oven for 45 minutes. Top each serving with a heaping teaspoon of cheese. Serves 2.

When increasing recipe, figure 2 eggs per person. Always monitor the buttermilk quantity so that it does not thin the eggs too much; they need to maintain their eggy consistency.

# EASY EGG SURPRISE

*Helen Tucker, Bed & Breakfast on the Park, Anchorage*

| | |
|---|---|
| 10 **eggs** | 1 tsp. **seasoning salt** |
| 1/2 cup **grated parmesan cheese** | 2 Tb. **medium salsa** |
| (or any cheese you like) | 1 Tb. **butter** |
| 1/4 cup **milk** | 1 lb. **frozen stir-fry vegetables** |

**M**ix eggs, cheese, milk, seasoning salt and salsa together; set aside. In hot skillet, add butter and vegetables. Cook until vegetables are thawed and cooked lightly. Add egg mixture and stir until eggs are done. Serve immediately. Serves 6 to 8.

The log "wing" of Bed & Breakfast On The Park was originally a church, built in 1946. The interior of the old church was remodeled in 1992 as guest bedrooms with private baths.

# EGGS MARVELOUS

*Norine Shandro, Bed & Breakfast Inn Margaree*
*Dawson Creek*

This is a great recipe to make the night before and bake the next morning.

1 cup **bacon, ham or sausage**
¹/₄ cup **chopped green onion**
2 Tb. **butter**
12 **eggs, scrambled,**
  **soft but not quite set**
1 10-oz. **can mushrooms, drained**
2 cups **bread crumbs**
3 Tb. **melted butter**
**paprika**

**Cheese sauce:**
2 Tb. **butter**
2 Tb. **flour**
2 cups **milk**
1¹/₂ cups **old cheese**

auté bacon, green onions and 2 Tb. butter and set aside. Next make cheese sauce: Melt 2 Tb. butter in saucepan over low heat. Add the flour, and stir for 2 minutes until well incorporated. Turn the heat to medium, and add the milk, stirring constantly until sauce bubbles. Remove from heat, add cheese and stir until melted. Fold eggs, mushrooms, bacon and onion into cheese sauce. Pour into buttered 9" x 12" baking dish. Combine bread crumbs and 3 Tb. melted butter, and pour over mixture. Sprinkle with paprika. Cover and refrigerate overnight. Bake for 40 minutes at 350°F. Serves 8.

# FIESTA BRUNCH

*Diane Schoming*
*Morning Glory Bed & Breakfast, Homer*

$1/2$ cup **soft butter**
8 slices **firm bread**
2 to 3 cups ($1/2$ to $3/4$ lb.) **grated jack cheese**
1 4-oz. can **diced green chilies**
$1/2$ lb. **bacon, cooked and diced**
6 **eggs**
2 cups **milk**
$1/2$ cup **half and half**
1 tsp. **dry mustard**
$1/2$ tsp. **Tabasco sauce**
1 Tb. **instant minced onions**
$1/2$ tsp. **salt**
**salsa**

**B**utter bread on both sides; cut into small cubes and spread evenly over bottom of lightly greased 9" x 13" baking dish. Sprinkle evenly with cheese, diced chilies and bacon.

Combine eggs with milk, half and half, and seasonings. Pour over bread mixture. Cover and refrigerate overnight. Bake uncovered for 45 minutes at 325°F. Serve with salsa, if desired. Serves 8.

# HAM AND CHEESE FLORENTINE

*Theresa Ely, Birch Grove Inn Bed and Breakfast*
*Fairbanks*

¹/₂ package **frozen puff-pastry sheet (1 sheet)**
1 **egg, beaten**
1 Tb. **water**
2 **green onions, chopped (about** ¹/₄ **cup)**
¹/₂ tsp. **dried oregano leaves, crushed**
¹/₂ lb. **cooked ham, sliced**
¹/₂ lb. **cooked turkey, sliced**
1 cup **spinach leaves**
4 oz. **Swiss cheese, sliced**

Thaw pastry at room temperature for 30 minutes. Preheat oven to 400°F. Mix egg and water, and set aside. Mix onions and oregano, and set aside. Unfold pastry on lightly floured surface. Roll into 12" x 16" rectangle. With short side facing you, layer ham, turkey, spinach and cheese on bottom half of pastry to within 1 inch of edge. Sprinkle with onion mixture. Starting at short side, roll into a jelly roll. Place seam side down on baking sheet. Tuck ends under to seal. Brush with egg mixture. Bake 25 minutes or until golden brown. Slice and serve warm. Serves 6.

# HEAVENLY FRENCH CUSTARD

*Christine & Corbett Upton*
*Applesauce Inn B&B, Fairbanks*

"One guest described this in the guestbook as a 'breakfast to die for,' hence the name."

1 loaf (1 lb.) **French baguette bread**
**light cream cheese**
**red raspberry jam**
8 **eggs**
3 cups **milk (I sometimes use 1 12-oz. can evaporated milk and 1¹/₂ cups of half and half)**
1 Tb. **vanilla (clear, if you have it)**
¹/₂ tsp. **salt**
**slivered almonds**
**butter**

**B**utter a 2-inch-tall, 10-inch casserole dish. Slice bread (minus ends) into 1¹/₂-inch slices, making a slit through the middle of the slices, and spread each with cream cheese and 1 Tb. jam. Use enough bread to make one layer in the casserole dish. Whisk eggs, milk, vanilla and salt, then pour mixture over bread. Cover and refrigerate overnight. In the morning, preheat oven to 350°F. Sprinkle slivered almonds on top of casserole and dot with butter. Bake uncovered for 30 to 40 minutes until puffed and golden. Serve with berry and/or maple syrup. Serves 8.

# HERBED HAM AND CHEESE BAKE

*Christine & Corbett Upton*
*Applesauce Inn B&B, Fairbanks*

"A truly original creation, this casserole is perfectly seasoned by using a high-quality, dense, herbed bread."

1 lb. **loaf of dense, herbed bread**
8 to 10 slices **Canadian bacon**
8 to 10 slices **white cheese**
   **(provolone, Swiss or Monterey Jack)**
8 **large eggs**
3 cups **milk**
1/2 cup **grated white cheese**

Cut loaf in half length-wise, trim ends off, then slice crosswise into 8 to 10 pairs of slices, 1-inch thick. Place one slice from each pair into a well-buttered 2-inch-tall by 10-inch casserole dish. Place a slice of Canadian bacon and cheese on each half piece of bread. Cover with other bread halves. Combine eggs and milk, and pour mixture over bread. Refrigerate covered overnight. Uncover and sprinkle with grated cheese. Bake at 350°F for 40 to 50 minutes, until puffed and golden. Serves 6.

# McKINLEY BREAKFAST

*Leicha Welton, 7 Gables Inn, Fairbanks*

²/₃ cup **chopped ham**
²/₃ cup **grated cheddar cheese**
1 Tb. **Dijon mustard**
1 Tb. **mayonnaise**
4 slices **whole wheat bread**
3 **eggs**
1¹/₂ cups **milk**

In medium bowl, combine ham, cheese, mustard and mayonnaise. Make 2 sandwiches using whole wheat bread slices, and ham and cheese mixture. Cut each sandwich diagonally into quarters. Place 2 sandwich triangles each—pointed end up (like mountain peaks)—into 4 oven-proof ramekins sprayed with nonstick cooking spray. In another bowl, combine eggs and milk. Pour equally over the 4 sandwich dishes, making sure the bread has been soaked. Refrigerate overnight and remove about three-quarters of an hour before baking. Bake in preheated 325°F oven for 30 minutes. Serves 4.

# MY DAD'S BAKED EGGS

*Ronald S. Pendleton, Journeymen's B&B, Homer*

**butter**
**7 slices processed cheese**
**6 eggs**
**milk OR cream**
**garlic salt**

Line a baking dish with butter. Put 6 slices of cheese on bottom of dish and crack eggs onto cheese. Pour a dot of milk or cream on each yolk. Crumble the other slice of cheese on top of the eggs, and season with garlic salt. Bake at 400°F for about 10 minutes, or until set. Serve with cornmeal muffins.

# NORTH COUNTRY GLACIER MELTER

*Cindy H. Kinard, North Country Castle Bed & Breakfast*
*Anchorage*

12 slices **wheat bread**
6 Tb. **butter**
11 Tb. **grated parmesan cheese, divided**
1 7-oz. can **diced mild chilies**
$^1/_2$ tsp. **diced jalapeño peppers**
6 **artichoke hearts (canned), chopped**
4 **large eggs, beaten 'til creamy yellow**
$2^1/_4$ cup **milk**
6 tsp. **diced pimiento**

Trim crusts from bread. Melt butter in microwave in a 9" x 13" casserole dish. Dip one side of 6 bread slices in the butter to cover lightly; set aside. Place remaining 6 slices in remaining butter in casserole. Top bread with mixture of 5 Tb. cheese, mild chilies, jalapeño peppers and artichokes. Place set-aside bread slices over cheese mixture, butter side up. Mix eggs and milk, and pour over bread stacks. Top each bread stack with 1 tsp. pimiento and 1 Tb. parmesan cheese. Cover and refrigerate 1 hour or overnight. Bake uncovered in preheated, 350°F oven for 45 minutes, or until knife inserted in center comes out clean. Serves 6.

# SAUSAGE STRATA ELEANOR

*LaVerne Wood, Eleanor's Northern Lights Bed & Breakfast, Fairbanks*

This is a good old standard. It is particularly good because it can be prepared the night before serving.

4 Tb. **butter**

8 slices **white bread, trimmed and quartered**

1 lb. **cheddar cheese (mild to sharp), shredded**

1 lb. **breakfast sausage, fried and diced**

2 cups **milk**

4 **eggs**

1 20-oz. can **cream of mushroom soup**

1/2 tsp. **dry mustard**

1/2 tsp. **salt**

1 small can **sliced mushrooms, or sautéed fresh mushrooms**

Layer the bread, cheese and sausage in a buttered 9" x 12" baking dish. You should get at least 2 layers. Mix milk, eggs, soup, mustard and salt, and pour over layers. Cover and let sit overnight in the refrigerator. Before baking, spread mushrooms on top. Bake at 350°F for approximately 1 hour. Check with knife for doneness: knife should be dry. Let cool 10 minutes before cutting. Serves 8 to 10.

# CHOCOLATE DROP B&B'S SAUSAGE STRATA

*Judy Ceglie, Chocolate Drop B&B, Homer*

7 slices **bread**
2 lbs. **sausage**
1 small can **sliced mushrooms, drained**
9 **eggs**
1 pint **half and half**
1/4 tsp. **salt**
3/4 tsp. **dry mustard**
2 Tb. **onion flakes**
2 cups **shredded sharp cheddar cheese**

Butter a 9" x 13" baking dish, and place bread on bottom of dish. Cook sausage, crumbling while stirring. Drain and place over bread. Layer mushrooms over sausage. Beat eggs, add cream, and then spices and onion flakes. Pour over sausage. Sprinkle cheese over top. Refrigerate overnight, if desired. Bake at 375°F for 45 minutes until brown and bubbly. Serves 12 to 15.

# SAUSAGE-CHEESE
# BREAKFAST STRATA

*Betty Heinrichs, Wintel's Bed and Breakfast, Kodiak*

10 cups cubed French bread (¹/₂- to ³/₄-inch pieces)
³/₄ cup fully cooked smoked sausage links, cut into ³/₄-inch pieces
1 4-oz. can mushroom stems and pieces, drained
1¹/₂ cups shredded sharp cheddar cheese
1 cup shredded Monterey Jack cheese with jalapeño peppers
7 eggs, beaten
3¹/₂ cups milk
2 Tb. snipped fresh chives
1 Tb. vinegar
¹/₂ tsp. salt
¹/₄ tsp. pepper
¹/₂ tsp. seasoned salt
2 tsp. dried marjoram, crushed
1 tsp. dry mustard

In two 2-quart, greased casseroles, put one half of bread cubes, sausage and mushrooms. Sprinkle with cheese. Top with remaining bread, sauage and mushrooms. Combine eggs, milk, chives, vinegar and seasonings. Divide evenly and pour over casseroles. Cover and refrigerate a minimum of 2 hours, or up to 48 hours. Bake uncovered at 325°F for 1 hour. Serves 12.

# Appetizers

The remains of Montague House, a typical early-day road-house, can be seen along the Klondike Highway, approximately 89 miles north of Whitehorse, Yukon Territory. A total of 52 stopping places on the winter trail between Whitehorse and Dawson City, offering lodging and meals to travelers, were listed in the Jan. 16, 1901, edition of the "Whitehorse Star." Montague House was listed at Mile 99 along the stagecoach route.

**Appetizers**

# SWISS CHEESE FONDUE

*Hap Wurlitzer, Hatcher Pass Lodge*
*Mile 17.5 Fishhook-Willow Road*

<sup></sup>

$1/2$ loaf **French bread**
$1/2$ **apple, sliced**
1 clove **garlic**
2 shots **white wine**
1 shot **cherry brandy (kirsch)**
5 oz. **grated Swiss Gruyere cheese**
5 oz. **grated Swiss Emmentaler cheese**
dash **black pepper**
dash **nutmeg**
1 tsp. **lemon juice**

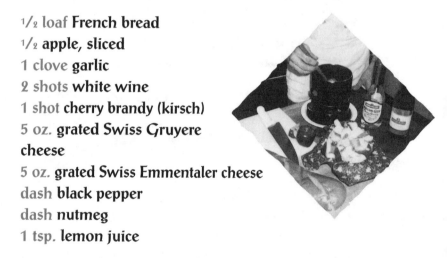

**C**ut bread into 1-inch squares with a portion of crust on each piece. (The crust holds onto the fondue fork as you dip into the cheese.) Ring a bread basket with apple slices and fill with the bread cubes.

Rub the fondue pan with the garlic clove, until it is crushed. Put in the shots of wine and brandy. Over a low heat, add the grated cheeses. With the end of a wooden spoon stir in a figure-8 pattern until the cheese is well-melted and of a smooth consistency. Add the pepper, nutmeg and lemon juice, continuing to mix into a smooth cheese. Serves 2 to 4.

# CRAB-STUFFED MUSHROOMS

*Deb Kremzar, Bitter Creek Cafe & Mercantile, Stewart*

1/4 cup **butter**
4 Tb. **minced onion**
1 large clove **garlic, crushed**
3 Tb. **flour**
1/2 to 3/4 cup **milk**
1 Tb. **fresh dill (or 1 tsp. dried)**
2 Tb. **fresh lemon juice**
**salt and pepper to taste**
1 to 1 1/2 cups **crab meat**
12 to 16 **white mushroom caps**
**grated parmesan cheese**
**garlic butter to taste**

elt butter in saucepan; add onion and garlic, and sauté. Add flour and cook over medium-low heat for 2 minutes. Add milk gradually, until you reach a fairly thick consistency. Add dill, lemon juice, salt and pepper. Add enough crab meat to sauce to hold it together. Stuff mushroom caps with crab mixture and sprinkle with grated parmesan cheese. Broil in garlic butter for 15 minutes or until mushrooms are cooked. Serves 6 to 8.

# DEEP-FRIED FIDDLEHEADS IN BEER BATTER

*Mary Carey, Mary's McKinley View Lodge*
*Mile 134.5 George Parks Highway*

"At Mary's McKinley View Lodge, I became noted for food that is different. Patrons often drove to my place all the way from Anchorage, and from towns and villages along the route, to eat my fiddlehead fern specialties.

"I became interested in working with ferns after homesteading in a fly-in area. For me the nearest supermarket was over a hundred miles away. Fresh greens were, and still are, a precious commodity."

1 qt. **fresh fiddleheads, 3-inch necks**
1 cup **flour**
2 tsp. **salt**
1 tsp. **pepper**

**Batter:**
4 egg **whites**
1 bottle **beer**
1 cup **flour**

 f fern is not completely dry, blot dry with paper towels. Put dry mixture into paper bag and shake a little of the fern at a time, as you would chicken.

For batter, beat egg whites until stiff. Add beer and flour. Whip until stiff. Dip fiddleheads into batter by holding tips of stems.

Appetizers

Deep fry until golden brown. (Excerpted with permission from "Let's Taste Alaska.")

Mary Carey has been extolling the virtues of the fiddlehead fern, in particular the ostrich fern (Matteuccia struthiopteris), since she was first introduced to the green while teaching school in Talkeetna in 1962. She also has the world's only fiddlehead fern farm (see photo below), located on the Talkeetna Spur Road. Fiddleheads are picked in early spring when the tightly coiled clusters resemble a fiddle's head. The ostrich fern is a favorite because of its flavor and because it has the least amount of flaky brown coating, which must be picked off before use. The ostrich fern is also distinguished by a central fertile frond that is surrounded by taller, green, sterile fronds. Fiddleheads should be served cooked.

# BOURSIN AU POIVRE

*Lynn Coutts, The Noland House, Atlin*

1 8-oz. package **cream cheese, room temperature**
1 clove **garlic, crushed**
1 tsp. **dill**
1 tsp. **caraway seeds**
1 tsp. **basil**
1 tsp. **chives, chopped**
**Lemon pepper to taste**

**B**lend cheese with all ingredients except lemon pepper. Pat into round, flattened shape between two layers of wax paper. Roll on all sides in lemon pepper. Refrigerate, covered. Keeps well for several days. Serve with bagels, crackers, etc. Serves 8.

# TURNAGAIN HOUSE MUSHROOMS

*Turnagain House, Mile 103.1 Seward Highway*

4 oz. chopped scallops
4 oz. chopped shrimp
1/2 lb. chopped mushroom stems
4 green onions, chopped
1 tsp. fresh tarragon
3 oz. white wine
1 oz. brandy
juice from 1/2 lemon

18 large mushroom caps
2 to 3 Tb. butter
salt
pepper
cayenne
3/4 lb. cream cheese
grated parmesan cheese
bread crumbs

Combine scallops, shrimp, mushroom stems, onions and tarragon; poach in white wine, brandy and lemon juice until seafood is cooked. Drain and chill. Sauté mushroom caps in butter, salt, pepper and cayenne to taste. Combine cream cheese with chilled scallop and shrimp mixture, and stuff mushroom caps. Top mushrooms with grated parmesan cheese and bread crumbs. Bake 20 minutes at 375°F. Serves 8 to 10.

# GUEST HOUSE SPECIAL

*Red Salmon Guest House, Mile 48.2 Sterling Highway*

**Herbed cream cheese:**
1/2 tsp. **chopped chives**
11/2 tsp. **chopped parsley**
2 tsp. **chopped whole green onion**
1 **small garlic clove, peeled**
3/4 tsp. **tarragon vinegar**
2 dashes **fresh, finely ground pepper**
62/3 oz. **cream cheese**

4 **bagels, halved and toasted**
4 dabs **herbed cream cheese**
4 handfuls **smoked salmon, crumbled**
1 **lemon**
**parsley**

lace all the ingredients for herbed cream cheese, except the cream cheese, into the bowl of a good food processor fitted with a steel S-blade. Process for 15 seconds. In a separate mixing bowl, combine the herb mixture and cream cheese, and beat thoroughly with an electric mixer. Herbed cream cheese can be refrigerated up to a week. (Note: If desired, reserve a tablespoon of the herb mixture and mix with 1/2 cup mayonnaise to use on sandwiches or hamburgers.)

Spread herbed cream cheese on toasted bagels. Sprinkle each bagel half with salmon; squeeze a bit of lemon juice on top; and sprinkle with chopped parsley. Garnish with lemon slices and sprigs of parsley. Serves 4.

**Beverages**

escribed as the "farthest north of the old-time Richardson trail hostelries," the ruins of the old Black Rapids Hunting Lodge may be seen at Mile V 227.4 Richardson Highway. The Richardson Highway began as a trail for gold stampeders in 1898 and became Alaska's first road—connecting Fairbanks with Valdez—when it was updated to automobile standards in the 1920s. A number of roadhouses that served the early traffic along the Richardson still exist, including Tsaina Lodge, Tiekel River Lodge, Tonsina Lodge, Copper Center Lodge and Paxson Lodge.

# CRANBERRY MINT PUNCH

*Mary Carey, Mary's McKinley View Lodge*
*Mile 134.5 Parks Highway*

4 cups **lowbush cranberry juice**
4 cups **water**
2 cups **pineapple juice**
2 cups **orange juice**
1/2 cup **sugar**
1/2 cup **mint sprigs**
1 **orange, thinly sliced**

Combine all ingredients except orange slices and mint. Mix well. Serve over ice. Garnish with a sprig of mint and orange slice. Prettier if orange slice is split to the center and hung over edge of glass. (Excerpted with permission from "Let's Taste Alaska.")

Octogenarian Mary Carey is an Alaska homesteader, author of 12 books, and runs not only the McKinley View Lodge but also the "world's only fiddlehead fern farm", located a mile off the Talkeetna Spur Road. Mary came to Alaska in 1963, and taught school in Talkeetna. She has also worked as a reporter, and had a weekly newspaper column.

# RASPBERRY-RHUBARB SPICED PUNCH

*Mary Carey, Mary's McKinley View Lodge*
*Mile 134.5 Parks Highway*

4 cups **raspberries**
4 cups **thinly sliced rhubarb**
1 cup **sugar**
3 sticks **cinnamon**
12 **whole cloves**
1 tsp. **nutmeg**
1 **lemon, sliced**
4 cups **freshly brewed tea**

Cook berries and rhubarb 3 minutes in just enough water to cover. Put through colander. Strain through cheesecloth into tea. Tie spices in cheesecloth and boil in tea for 5 minutes. Serve hot with dash of nutmeg and a lemon slice. (Excerpted with permission from "Let's Taste Alaska.")

# MULLED WINE

*Sharon Waisanen, Spruce Avenue Bed & Breakfast*
*Kenai Spur Highway*

"We serve this to guests during the holidays or for ourselves on a blustery, snowy Alaskan night."

1 cup **sugar**
2 to 3 **sticks cinnamon**
12 **whole allspice**
1 cup **water**
12 **whole cloves**
1 **lemon**
3 cups **red wine**

 immer everything but wine for 5 minutes. Let stand 30 minutes. Add wine, heat until just under boiling.

# ORANGE JUICE SPECIAL
*Rose Ringstad, Rose's Forget-Me-Not B&B, Fairbanks*

¹/₂ 16-oz. **package frozen strawberries**
1 12-oz. can **frozen orange juice**
**Fresh strawberries**

Cut 16-oz. package of frozen strawberries in half lengthwise, then chop one of the halves into 8 pieces. Combine concentrated orange juice and frozen strawberries in blender and add water to fill blender. Blend at medium speed for 30 to 40 seconds. Stir and serve while still frosty and frothy, topping each glass with a fresh strawberry. Serves 6.

# Breads

anley Roadhouse, in Manley Hot Springs at Mile 152 Elliott Highway, has been serving Alaska since 1906. One of Alaska's oldest original roadhouses, the Manley Roadhouse offers "traditional Alaska home-style hospitality" and "good food." It is located on Manley Slough in a field of irises. It is a community gathering place for local miners, trappers, dog mushers and fishermen. The roadhouse has some wonderful prehistoric fossils on display that were unearthed by miners.

# ALASKA BACKPACK MOUNTAIN BREAD

*Jan Thacker*
*Coldfoot Services and Arctic Acres Inn, Coldfoot*

"This bread will keep for 3 weeks. It is almost a meal and very high in energy."

4 cups **whole wheat flour**
1 cup **water**
³/₄ cup **brown sugar**
¹/₂ cup **honey**
¹/₃ cup **wheat germ**
¹/₃ cup **vegetable oil**
¹/₄ cup **sesame seed**
¹/₄ cup **molasses**
3 Tb. **dry milk powder**
1¹/₂ tsp. **salt**
1¹/₂ tsp. **baking soda**

**M**ix all ingredients until smooth. Pour into greased 8" x 8" x 2" pan. Bake at 300°F for about 1 hour, or until bread pulls away from sides of pan. Cool and cut into 16 equal squares. Makes 1 loaf.

# "NUTS ABOUT BANANA" BREAD

*Christine and Corbett Upton*
*Cedar Creek Inn, Fairbanks*

"I was not a banana bread fan until I found this recipe. Even though Cedar Creek Inn vacation home guests do their own cooking, I often send over a loaf with their breakfast stock."

1 cup **sugar**
1 Tb. **molasses**
$^1/_2$ cup **vegetable oil**
2 **eggs**
1 Tb. **plain yogurt**
3 **bananas, mashed**
1 tsp. **lemon juice**
2 tsp. **baking powder**
$^1/_4$ tsp. **salt**
2 cups **flour**
$^1/_2$ tsp. **baking soda**
1 cup **coarse nuts**

ix well the first 9 ingredients. Add flour, baking soda and lastly the nuts. Pour batter into greased loaf pan. Bake 1 hour at 375°F, until loaf tests done.

# LAKE HOUSE BED & BREAKFAST BUBBLE BREAD

*Marilyn Talmage, Lake House Bed & Breakfast, Valdez*

2 packages **active dry yeast**
1 cup **granulated sugar**
$^1/_2$ cup **warm water (100° to 115°F)**
2 sticks (1 cup) **softened sweet butter or margarine**
$1^1/_2$ Tb. **salt**
1 cup **warm milk**
3 **eggs, plus 2 egg yolks**
6 to 7 cups **all-purpose flour**
$^1/_2$ cup **brown sugar**
$^1/_2$ cup **dried cranberries, dried cherries or raisins**

Combine the yeast, white sugar and water in a large mixing bowl. While this is proofing, stir 1 stick of the butter and the salt into the warm milk. Add to the yeast mixture. Stir in all the eggs. Beat with a wooden spoon to blend thoroughly. Add the flour, 1 cup at a time, stirring well after each addition. Turn dough out on a floured board and knead, adding more flour as needed until the dough is no longer sticky. Knead a full 10 minutes, until the dough is elastic and pliable. Shape into a ball and put in a buttered bowl, turning to coat all over with butter. Cover with plastic wrap and set in a warm, draft-free place to rise until doubled in bulk. Punch the dough down and let rest for 5

**Breads**

minutes. Turn out on a lightly floured board and again shape into a ball. Let rest for another 5 to 10 minutes. While the dough is resting, butter a 10-inch tube pan.

In a saucepan, melt the second stick of sweet butter with the brown sugar and cranberries. Pinch off enough dough to make golf ball-sized balls. Roll the balls in the butter mixture and place in bottom of the tube pan arranging balls in loose layers. Pour what is left of the butter mixture over the top. Cover loosely with a foil tent and let the dough rise to the top of the tube pan. Bake in a preheated 375°F oven for about 1 hour. When bread is ready, the top will sound hollow when tapped. Unmold and let cool thoroughly before slicing, or serve warm and pull apart. Yields 1 ring loaf.

# SHIRLEY'S HERB FOCCACIA

*M.M. Clay, Sportsman's Kispiox Lodge, Hazelton*

3 tsp. **yeast**
1/2 tsp. **sugar**
21/2 cups **warm water, divided**
11/2 cups **milk OR sour milk**
1 tsp. **salt**
1/2 cup **oil**
1 tsp. **oregano**
1/2 cup **parmesan cheese**
7 cups **flour**

Dissolve yeast and sugar in 1/2 cup warm water. Mix together 2 cups warm water, milk, salt, oil, oregano, parmesan cheese, flour and the dissolved yeast mixture. Knead. Let rise in bowl for 1/2 hour; punch down, divide into 4 parts and put in 4 greased, round cake pans. Let rise for 1/2 hour. Dimple the surface with your fingertips and sprinkle with coarse salt. Bake in 350°F oven for 1/2 hour.

# SOURDOUGH FRENCH BREAD

*Gail Corbin, Lisianski Inlet Lodge, Pelican*

1¹/₂ cups **sourdough starter**
1¹/₂ cups **warm water**
1 Tb. **sugar**
1 Tb. **yeast**
2 tsp. **salt**
5 cups **flour**
¹/₂ tsp. **baking soda**

Mix in large bowl sourdough starter, water, sugar, yeast and salt. Let it set to dissolve yeast for 3 minutes. Add 3 or more cups of flour to make a thick batter. Raise until double in bulk. Add 1 cup flour with baking soda. Turn out and knead. Cut into 2 balls. Rest for 10 minutes. Shape into long, skinny loaves on cookie sheet buttered and coated with corn meal. Slash across top. Raise. Bake at 425°F for 15 minutes. Brush with salted water. Bake at 375°F for 20 to 30 minutes, or until done (sounds hollow when tapped on bottom). Makes 2 loaves.

# TWO-TONE BREAD

*Camp Denali and North Face Lodge, Denali National Park*

"In this popular dinner bread, two colors of dough form an attractive spiral."

3 cups **lukewarm water**

$1/2$ cup **honey**

2 Tb. **active dry yeast**

$31/2$ cups **unbleached white flour**

$1/2$ cup **nonfat powdered milk**

$1/2$ cup **vegetable oil**

2 tsp. **salt**

$1/2$ cup **bran**

2 cups **unbleached white flour**

$1/4$ cup **molasses**

2 Tb. **instant coffee granules**

$21/2$ cups **whole wheat flour**

1 cup **unbleached white flour**

**M**ix together water and honey; add yeast. When yeast mixture is foamy, add $31/2$ cups white flour, powdered milk, vegetable oil and salt. Stir vigorously, about 200 strokes. Divide dough in half. To one half gradually stir in bran and 2 cups white flour. To the other half, stir in molasses, coffee granules, wheat flour and 1 cup white flour. Knead each half separately, adding additional white flour as necessary until doughs are smooth and elastic. Place doughs in separate oiled bowls,

**Breads**

cover and let rise in a warm place until doubled in bulk. Punch down and divide each dough in half.

Roll out one piece of light dough into an 8" x 12" rectangle. Repeat with a piece of dark dough. Place one colored dough atop the other and roll out together into a larger rectangle, about 10" x 15", taking care to press out any air bubbles between layers. Roll up from the short side. Pinch seams together and place seam-side-down in a greased loaf pan. Repeat process with the two remaining pieces of dough. Cover and let rise in a warm place until almost doubled. Bake at 350°F for 40 to 45 minutes. Makes 2 5" x 9" loaves.

Founded in 1951, Camp Denali was one of Denali National Park's first wilderness vacation lodges. It is also a nature center, specializing in natural history and guided hiking activities, with special programs on Northern studies. The rustic, hand-crafted cabins cluster around a centralized dining room lodge. Camp Denali is located about a mile from North Face Lodge.

# SOURDOUGH PAUL'S BANANA NUT BREAD

*Paul Miebs, Sourdough Paul's Bed and Breakfast*
*Mile 193 George Parks Highway*

See Paul's sourdough starter method on opposite page. No sourdough sponge is necessary for this recipe.

1 cup **sugar**
¹/₃ cup **vegetable oil**
2 **eggs**, **beaten**
¹/₂ cup **sourdough starter**
2 cups **all-purpose flour**
1 tsp. **salt**
1 tsp. **baking soda**
3 **ripe bananas, mashed**
²/₃ cup **chopped walnuts**

**M**ix sugar and oil together. Beat in the eggs. Gently fold in the sourdough starter. Add together all the remaining ingredients. Preheat oven to 375°F. Bake in greased and floured bread pan in the center of oven for 40 to 50 minutes or until inserted toothpick comes out clean. Cool on rack.

**Breads**

## Starter:
3 medium potatoes, peeled and cut into pieces
3 cups water
1 package active yeast
1¹/₂ Tb. sugar, divided
2 cups flour, all-purpose unbleached preferred

oil potatoes in water until soft. Save the potato water for the starter; use the potatoes for dinner. Pour just 2 cups potato water into a glass bowl. Let cool until lukewarm. Mix the yeast and ¹/₂ Tb. sugar into potato water. Let stand until yeast is working (light and frothy looking). Add 2 cups flour and 1 Tb. sugar, and then mix it up good. Now cover bowl with towel, and let it set in a warm place for 3 days or more, until it is really bubbly looking. Be sure to stir the starter mixture each day. After 3 days, your new starter is ready for use in recipes.

Never store your starter in a plastic or metal container! Always use glass or pottery. Store starter in a cool place; the refrigerator if you have the luxury. Don't tightly seal your starter, as it needs air to breathe and grow. Sprinkle a little sugar on top to aid in the fermenting process when storing. If the water starts to separate in your starter, don't pour it off, just mix it back in and keep in a cool place. If a crust begins to appear on the surface, don't worry, just set it out at room temperature, and it will dissolve back into itself. Do not get salt into the starter at any cost. Salt kills sourdough! Do not use self-rising flour. Be sure to use your starter at least once every 2 weeks or more. Key secret: Use it or lose it.

# ALASKA CRANBERRY MUFFINS

*Pat Dwinnell, Longmere Lake Lodge B&B, Soldotna*

"I have been serving these to our family and friends for the past 20-plus years we have lived in Alaska. Since opening our lodge, I now serve them to our guests, and everyone likes them."

1¹/₄ cups **flour**
¹/₂ cup **sugar**
1 Tb. **baking powder**
¹/₄ tsp. **salt**
1 Tb. **grated, dried orange peel**
2 cups **all-bran cereal**
1¹/₄ cups **milk**
1 **egg**
¹/₄ cup **vegetable oil**
1 cup **lowbush cranberries**

ift together flour, sugar, baking powder, salt and orange peel, and set aside. In a large bowl, combine cereal, milk, egg and oil. Let it set for 5 minutes and then beat together. Add flour mixture, stirring only until combined. Add lowbush cranberries, dusted with 1 Tb. flour, and fold into the batter without breaking open the berries. I add them right from the freezer. Pour batter into muffin tins that have been sprayed with nonstick spray. Bake at 400°F for about 20 minutes. Makes 12 large muffins.

# CRAISIN PUFFIN MUFFINS

*Sandy Schroth, A Puffin's Bed & Breakfast, Gustavus*

2 cups **all-bran cereal**
1 cup **milk**
¹/₄ cup **oil, melted butter or margarine**
1 egg, **beaten**
¹/₄ cup **crushed pineapple, not drained**
¹/₃ cup **dried cranberries**
¹/₄ cup **sugar**
1¹/₄ cups **all-purpose flour**
1 Tb. **baking powder**
¹/₄ tsp. **salt**
¹/₄ tsp. **cinnamon (optional)**

Combine cereal and milk in a small bowl, and let stand for 5 minutes. Add oil, egg, pineapple and dried cranberries, and set aside. In a large bowl, combine sugar, flour, baking powder, salt and cinnamon. Add ingredients from the small bowl to the ingredients in the large bowl. Mix only until moistened. Add a little more pineapple juice if the batter looks too dry. Grease muffin tins, or use paper wrappers. Fill muffin tins ²/₃ full. Bake at 400°F for 15 minutes or until lightly browned. Makes 16 muffins.

# CRANBERRY BANANA BREAD/MUFFINS

*Geraldine Jauhola, Finnish Alaskan Bed & Breakfast*
*Mile 302.1 George Parks Highway*

³/₄ cup **fresh or frozen cranberries, chopped**
1 cup **sugar, divided in half**
1 tsp. **grated orange peel**

| | |
|---|---|
| 1³/₄ **cups flour** | 2 **eggs** |
| 2 tsp. **baking powder** | ³/₄ cup **mashed banana (2 small)** |
| ¹/₂ tsp. **baking soda** | ¹/₃ cup **vegetable oil** |
| ¹/₂ tsp. **salt** | ¹/₂ cup **chopped walnuts** |

In a small mixing bowl, combine cranberries, ¹/₂ cup of the sugar, and orange peel. Set aside. In large mixing bowl, sift together flour, remaining ¹/₂ cup of sugar, baking powder, baking soda and salt. In medium mixing bowl, combine eggs, bananas and oil; stir well with fork to combine. Add banana mixture to dry ingredients, stirring just enough to moisten. Stir in cranberry mixture and walnuts. Pour into well-greased and floured or parchment-lined 9" x 5" x 3" loaf pan, or lined muffin pan. Bake in preheated 350°F oven for 1 hour (bread) or 16 to 20 minutes (muffins). Done when golden brown and toothpick inserted in center comes out clean. Remove from pan and cool on rack. Serves 6.

# GREEN APPLE MUFFINS

*Ed & Dana Klinkhart*
*Snowline Bed & Breakfast, Anchorage*

2 cups **sugar**
1¹/₂ cups **vegetable oil**
3 **eggs, beaten**
2 tsp. **vanilla**
3 cups **flour**
1 tsp. **baking soda**
1 tsp. **salt**
3 cups **grated, unpeeled green apples (2 large)**
1 cup **chopped walnuts**

In a large mixing bowl, mix together sugar and oil. Add beaten eggs and vanilla. Stir in dry ingredients. Mixture will be thick. Fold in grated apples and nuts. Blend well. Pour into lined muffin tin. Bake at 350° for 20 to 25 minutes for regular muffins, or for 35 to 40 minutes for extra large "mega" muffins. Check with a toothpick for doneness. Makes 12 to 14 mega muffins.

# HEARTSTONE MUFFINS

*Jan Guertin, Jan's View Bed & Breakfast, Juneau*

"This recipe makes a gallon of batter, and it will keep in the refrigerator for up to 6 weeks. Just use as needed."

5 cups **sifted flour**
3 cups **sugar**
12 oz. **raisin bran cereal**
5 tsp. **baking soda**
2 tsp. **salt**
1 tsp. **cinnamon**
1/2 tsp. **allspice**
4 **beaten eggs**
1 qt. **buttermilk**
1 cup **oil**

Preheat oven to 350°F. Mix dry ingredients together. Add eggs, buttermilk and oil. Fill greased muffin tins 2/3 full. Bake 15 minutes or until golden brown. Makes 6 to 7 dozen.

# MARVELOUS MUFFINS

*Leicha Welton, 7 Gables Inn, Fairbanks*

¹/₂ cup **sugar**
¹/₃ cup **orange juice**
¹/₂ cup **butter**
1 cup **sugar**
¹/₂ cup **oil**
1¹/₂ cups **plain yogurt**
4 cups **flour**
2 tsp. **baking soda**
2 tsp. **salt**
2 tsp. **grated orange peel**
1 cup **raisins**
1 cup **chopped walnuts**

Combine ¹/₂ cup sugar and orange juice; set aside for topping. Cream butter, 1 cup sugar and oil, then blend in the yogurt. Combine dry ingredients and add them to the creamed mixture, stirring just until the ingredients are combined. Stir in grated orange peel, raisins and nuts. The batter will be stiff. Place in muffin tins, filling cups ³/₄ full. Bake at 350°F for 15 minutes. While warm, dip top of each muffin into sugar-orange juice mixture. Makes 2 dozen muffins.

# MIDNIGHT SUN MUFFINS

*Gail M. LaRocque*
*Cinnamon Cache Bakery & Coffee Shop, Carcross*

"I use applesauce instead of oil to make low-fat muffins."

2 cups **whole wheat flour**
1 cup **sugar**
2 tsp. **baking soda**
2 cups **grated carrots OR apples**
1/3 cup **chopped dry apricots**
1/3 cup **sunflower seeds**
1/3 cup **raisins**
1 **banana, mashed**
3 **eggs**
1 cup **oil OR applesauce**
2 tsp. **vanilla**

Combine dry ingredients and mix well. Stir in fruit and nuts. Beat together eggs, oil and vanilla. Stir into flour mixture until moistened. Spoon into muffin tins, and bake at 375°F for 15 to 20 minutes. Makes 15 large muffins.

# MOM'S MUFFINS

*Reva Jurgeleit, Cedarvale Cafe, Yellowhead Highway 16*

6 **eggs**
1 cup **sugar**
1 cup **walnuts**
1 cup **raisins**
1 cup **grated carrot**
1¹/₃ cups **vegetable oil**
1 can **crushed pineapple**
1 Tb. **cinnamon**
2 cups **bran**
4 cups **flour**
4 tsp. **baking powder**
1 tsp. **baking soda**

Beat eggs and sugar well. Add walnuts, raisins and grated carrot; mix well. Add oil, pineapple and cinnamon; mix well. Add bran and flour; mix well. Add baking powder and baking soda; mix well. Pour evenly into 2 muffin tins. Bake at 375°F for 35 minutes. Makes 2 dozen.

# PUMPKIN MUFFINS

*Susan and Ken Risse*
*The Blue Goose Bed & Breakfast, Fairbanks*

"Every fall I freeze a bunch of pumpkin. I cut the pumpkin in pieces, and bake at 350°F until a fork goes in easily. I then cut away the skin and purée the pumpkin in the food processor with the steel blade. Measure 1 cup, put in a small plastic bag and freeze. This is one of my most asked-for recipes, and the thing that makes it is the fresh frozen pumpkin."

| | |
|---|---|
| 1 cup **mashed pumpkin (fresh frozen)** | 1 tsp. **baking soda** |
| 1/2 cup **oil** | 1/4 tsp. **nutmeg** |
| 1/4 cup **water** | 1/4 tsp. **cinnamon** |
| 2 **eggs** | 1/4 tsp. **allspice** |
| 1 cup **sugar** | 1/2 cup **berries** |
| 1 1/2 cups **flour** | 1/2 cup **chopped nuts** |
| 1/2 tsp. **salt** | |

**M**ix pumpkin, oil, water, eggs and sugar in one bowl. Mix flour, salt, baking soda, nutmeg, cinnamon and all-spice in another bowl. Combine two mixtures. Add berries and nuts. Pour batter into muffin tins and sprinkle fairly heavily with cinnamon sugar. Bake at 350°F for 25 minutes. Makes 12 muffins.

# SOURDOUGH BLUEBERRY MUFFINS

*Carla Pitzel*
*Hawkins House Bed and Breakfast, Whitehorse*

Set the sponge at least 6 to 8 hours before making these muffins (see Sourdough Starter recipe on page 86 for sponge directions).

1½ cups **whole-wheat flour**
½ cup **sugar**
1 tsp. **salt**
¼ cup **nonfat dry milk**
1 **egg**
½ cup **melted butter or vegetable oil**
**Sourdough sponge**
¾ cup **blueberries**
1 tsp. **baking soda**
1 Tb. **water**

ift flour, sugar, salt and nonfat dry milk into a bowl. Make a well in the center. Mix egg and butter thoroughly into sponge. Add this to the well in the flour. Stir only enough to moisten the flour mixture. Add blueberries. Dissolve soda in water. Add this mixture to the batter just before filling the muffin tins. Fill greased muffin tins ¾ full. Bake in 375°F oven for 30 to 35 minutes. Yields 20 small or 12 large muffins.

# SOURDOUGH STARTER AND SPONGE

*Carla Pitzel, Hawkins House Bed and Breakfast, Whitehorse*

"Sourdough isn't for a beginner cook, but it's a fun challenge for an experienced one. This yeast-based starter makes it easier. If you want to make a real starter, omit the yeast and add 4 Tb. sugar and 1¹/₂ tsp. salt to the start and it will sour the same, only it takes about 5 days. If you make it this way, you will need fresh-ground, organic flour and pure water (which hasn't been chlorinated or treated), otherwise it may not work."

## Sourdough Starter:

2 cups **flour**

1 tsp. **salt**

3 Tb. **sugar**

¹/₂ tsp. **yeast**

2 cups **warm water**

Take a gallon crock and add all ingredients. Stir mixture until it is a smooth, thin paste. Cover with lid and set in a warm place on the kitchen counter to sour. Stir it several times a day. In 2 or 3 days your sourdough will be ready. This is your Sourdough Starter. Now you are ready to make your Sponge. (Your starter will keep indefinitely in a clean, covered glass container in the refrigerator. Never use a metal container or leave a metal spoon in the starter or sponge. If unused for several weeks, the starter may need to sit out an extra night before adding the flour and water for the sponge.)

## Sourdough Sponge:

2 cups **flour**
1 Tb. **sugar**
¹/₂ tsp. **salt**
2 cups **water**

Make the sponge the night before you want to make your muffins. Add all ingredients to the starter and beat well. Set in a warm place, free from draft, to develop overnight. In the moning, the sponge will have gained half again its bulk and will be covered with air bubbles. It will have a pleasant yeasty odor.

# HOMEMADE BUNS

*Harmke DeBruin, Spirit Lake Wilderness Resort*
*Mile 72.3 Klondike Highway*

16 cups **flour**
4 Tb. **yeast**
4 **eggs**
6 Tb. **sugar**
12 Tb. **oil**
6 cups **lukewarm water**
**salt to taste**

In a large bowl mix 12 cups flour and yeast. In another bowl mix eggs, sugar, oil, water and salt. Combine together using a wooden spoon. Add the other 4 cups of flour to the mixture. The dough is right when it doesn't stick to your hands anymore. Cover the dough with a towel and let it rise in a warm place for 30 minutes. Punch it down with your fingers and let it rise for another 30 minutes. Put the dough in pans (you can make either buns or loaves) and let it rise another hour. Let it bake for 20 to 25 minutes at 350°F. If you want low-calorie buns, then don't use the sugar. Makes large 25 buns.

# ORANGE RYE ROLLS

*Camp Denali and North Face Lodge*
*Denali National Park*

| | |
|---|---|
| 1¹/₄ cups **lukewarm water** | 1¹/₂ cups **whole-wheat flour** |
| ¹/₃ cup **molasses** | ¹/₂ cup **vegetable oil** |
| 2 Tb. **honey** | 3 **eggs** |
| 2 Tb. **active dry yeast** | ³/₄ tsp. **baking soda** |
| ³/₄ cup **orange juice concentrate** | 1 tsp. **salt** |
| 1 Tb. **finely grated orange rind** | 3 cups **unbleached white** |
| 1¹/₂ cups **rye flour** | **flour (approximately)** |

**M**ix together water, molasses and honey. Add yeast. When yeast mixture is foamy, add orange juice concentrate, orange rind, rye flour, whole wheat flour, vegetable oil, 2 of the eggs, baking soda and salt. Stir vigorously, about 200 strokes. Gradually stir in enough white flour to form a soft dough. Knead until smooth. Place in an oiled bowl, cover and let rise in a warm place until doubled in bulk. Punch down and shape into rolls. Place on a greased baking sheet, about ¹/₂ inch apart. Cover and let rise until very light and almost doubled. (Rye rolls take extra rising time.) Brush with a mixture of the remaining egg (beaten) and 1 Tb. water. Bake rolls for 20 to 25 minutes at 350°F. The bottoms overbrown easily, so watch carefully during baking. Makes about 3 dozen rolls.

# POTATO ROLLS

*Vilma Anderson*
*McKinley Foothills Bed & Breakfast, Trapper Creek*

1 **medium potato**
1 package **yeast**
1 cup **warm milk (canned milk works better)**
2 Tb. **sugar**
2 tsp. **salt**
1/2 stick **butter**
2 **beaten eggs (at room temperature)**
41/2 to 51/2 cups **flour (you can mix some oatmeal flour with the white)**

**B**oil potato and save the water. Mix 1 cup potato water with yeast and some flour. Mix well and let stand a few minutes. Mash the potato, and add it to yeast mixture, along with milk, sugar, salt, butter and eggs. Add flour a little bit at a time, until bread dough is elastic and not too sticky. Let it rise until doubled in size. Punch down. Take a chunk and turn it on a floured board and make a flat piece like a pizza. Cut into triangles: first half, then quarters, etc., until it is all cut up into small triangles. Roll them one at a time. Place in a greased baking dish (you can use nonstick spray). Bake for 15 minutes, or until done, at 375°F. Makes 6 to 8. These buns can be frozen, and recipe can be doubled and tripled. Fast yeast can be used, too.

**Breads**

# SOUR CREAM ROLLS

*Bob-Lee, Manley Roadhouse, Manley Hot Springs*

1 package **yeast**
$^1/_2$ cup **warm water**
$^3/_4$ cup **shortening or butter, softened**
2 **eggs**
1 cup **sour cream at room temperature**
6 cups **flour**
$1^1/_2$ tsp. **salt**
$^1/_2$ cup **sugar**

Preheat oven to 375°F. Dissolve yeast in warm water. Mix together shortening, eggs and sour cream. Add to yeast mixture. Sift together flour, salt and sugar. Add to preceding ingredients. Lightly knead and let rise 1 hour. Shape into rolls. Let rise again, and bake until lightly brown, about 25 minutes. Makes about 4 dozen.

# EASY CINNAMON ROLLS

*Rita Gittins*
*Alaskan Frontier Gardens Bed and Breakfast, Anchorage*

**24** frozen dinner rolls
**1 3-oz. package** cook-and-serve vanilla pudding
**1 cup** brown sugar
**$^1/_2$ cup** sugar
**4 tsp.** cinnamon
**$^1/_2$ cup** chopped pecans (optional)
**$^1/_2$ cup** melted butter (1 cube)

Place 24 frozen dinner rolls in a well-greased bundt pan. Mix together vanilla pudding and brown sugar; pour over rolls. Combine sugar, cinnamon and optional pecans and sprinkle over rolls. Pour melted butter over all. Put bundt pan in oven to rise overnight. In the morning, bake at 350°F for 30 minutes. Let cool for 10 minutes in pan. Turn over on plate, cut and enjoy. Makes 2 dozen.

# OVERNIGHT CINNAMON ROLLS

*Diane Schoming, Morning Glory Bed & Breakfast, Homer*

1 package **frozen dinner rolls (about 10 to 15 rolls, or enough to fill the bottom of pan)**
1 3¹/₂-oz. package **instant butterscotch pudding**
1 cup **firmly packed brown sugar**
2 Tb. **cinnamon**
¹/₂ cup **melted butter**
¹/₂ cup **pecans**

Layer ingredients in a greased bundt cake pan in the following order: frozen rolls, pudding powder, brown sugar, cinnamon, butter and pecans. Cover the pan with foil topped with a clean towel and allow to sit overnight. Bake in a 350°F oven for 30 minutes. Serves 8 to 10.

# FROSTED CINNAMON ROLLS

*Carol Rhoades, Gracious House, Mile 82 Denali Highway*

**Rolls:**
4 to 5 cups **flour**
1 oz. (or 2 packages) **powdered yeast**
1 cup **milk**
¹/₃ cup **sugar**
¹/₃ cup **butter**
1 tsp. **salt**
2 **eggs**
¹/₃ cup **brown sugar**
¹/₃ cup **white sugar**
1¹/₂ Tb. **cinnamon**
**raisins** (optional)
**chopped pecans** (optional)

Combine 2 cups flour and yeast, and set aside. In saucepan, heat to milk, ¹/₃ cup sugar, butter and salt to 115°F; don't scald. Add to flour and yeast mixture, and stir. Add eggs and enough of remaining flour to make dough smooth and elastic. Press dough into greased bowl and let double. Cut dough in half and let it rest for 10 minutes. Roll out each half into a rectangle. Spread each with melted butter and top with brown sugar, white sugar and cinnamon, sprinkling evenly and adding raisins and chopped nuts, if desired. Roll up jelly-roll-style and cut each into 8 pieces. Put pieces into pan, cut-side down and with your

**Breads**

hand smash rolls half-way down. Let rise 45 minutes. Bake at 350°F for 20 to 25 minutes. While still warm, top with cream cheese frosting (see recipe following). Yields 16 rolls.

**Frosting:**
1 3-oz. package **cream cheese, softened**
1 Tb. **butter**
1 tsp. **vanilla**
2 cups **powdered sugar**

**W**ith an electric mixer at low speed, beat together cream cheese, butter and vanilla. Add sugar gradually, mixing until fluffy.

# VICTORIAN HEIGHTS CINNAMON ROLLS

*Phil and Tammy Clay*
*Victorian Heights Bed & Breakfast, Homer*

**Dough:**
1/2 cup **warm water**
1 Tb. **yeast**
1 tsp. **sugar**
21/2 cups **scalded milk**
1 cup **sugar**
11/2 tsp. **salt**
1/2 cup **margarine**
2 **eggs, beaten**
7 to 8 cups **flour**

**Filling:**
1/2 cup **margarine or butter, melted**
1 cup **brown sugar**
2 tsp. **cinnamon**
**nuts and raisins (optional)**

Stir water, yeast and sugar together and let set for 10 min-utes. In a separate bowl, mix scalded milk, sugar, salt and margarine; let stand until cooled, then add eggs and flour. Add the yeast mixture to this. (You can let this dough stand covered overnight in the refrigerator, or roll it out after mixing. I have found it easier to mix at night and roll out in the morning. It not only saves preparation time in the morning, but the dough is also easier to work with if it has been refrigerated. This is a very soft, sticky dough, but the soft dough means the rolls will be light.)

Roll out dough on a floured surface; pastry cloth works the best. Pour melted margarine or butter over the rolled out dough. Mix the brown sugar and cinnamon, and sprinkle over buttered dough. Add optional nuts and raisins, if you like.

Roll up dough from the long side and pinch to seal. Cut into 1-inch pieces with dental floss. (Yes, dental floss.) Take a string about 8 inches long and loop it under the end of the dough. Hold the ends of the floss above the dough, and cross over the ends of the floss until it cuts the dough. The floss won't squish and mash the dough like cutting with a knife will. Put pieces side by side in greased cake pan. To make rolls a little lighter, let them rise. Bake at 350°F for 20 to 25 minutes. Makes 2 dozen rolls.

# SOURDOUGH CINNAMON BUNS

*Grete Perkins,*
*Trapper John's Bed and Breakfast, Talkeetna*

"Finger lickin' good!"

1/4 cup **sugar**
1 cup **flour**
2 tsp. **baking powder**
1/4 tsp. **baking soda**
1/4 tsp. **salt**
1/4 cup **oil**
1 cup **sourdough starter**
3 Tb. **melted butter**
3/4 cup **brown sugar**
1 tsp. **cinnamon**

Mix together sugar, flour, baking powder and baking soda. Add salt, oil and sourdough starter. Knead dough for several minutes. Form dough into a ball, and turn out onto a floured board. Pat into a 9" x 12" rectangle. Brush with melted butter and sprinkle with brown sugar and cinnamon. Roll up and cut into 12 1-inch slices. Place in a greased 9" round pan. Bake at 425°F for 25 minutes, or until golden brown. Makes 12.

# CHEESE SCONES

*Wenda Lythgoe, The Cabin Bed & Breakfast*
*Km 219 Haines Highway*

4 Tb. **butter**
1 Tb. **honey**
1/2 cup **plain yogurt OR sour cream**
1 **egg**
1 1/4 cups **all-purpose flour**
1/2 cup **whole-wheat flour**
1/2 tsp. **baking powder**
1/2 tsp. **baking soda**
1/4 tsp. **salt**
1/2 cup **grated cheese**

Preheat oven to 400°F. Place rack in center of oven. Melt butter and honey together, and mix in yogurt and egg. In a medium-size bowl, mix together the flours, baking powder, baking soda and salt. Stir in cheese. Pour egg and yogurt mixture over flour mixture and combine gently with a fork. Don't over mix. Turn out onto a lightly floured surface and fold ingredients together gently a few times. Form into a 6- or 7-inch circle, 1-inch thick. Cut into 6 to 8 pie-shaped wedges and place on ungreased baking pan. Bake 12 to 15 minutes until lightly browned and puffed. Serve immediately with butter and homemade jam.

# DOT'S FAMOUS RASPBERRY SCONES

*Dot Keith*

*A Fireweed Hideaway Bed and Breakfast, Fairbanks*

"You can use any type of preserves. Instead of making an indentation and adding preserves, you can add chopped-up fruit to the dry ingredients before adding the milk and egg mixture. Then brush with egg white, and add slivered almonds and granulated sugar on the top. Let your imagination run wild. This is a good, basic recipe and the most moist scone I have tried. I freeze them individually in zip-lock bags, and then defrost and reheat in an electric bun warmer to serve at our bed and breakfast."

4 cups **all-purpose flour**

³/₄ cup **sugar**

3 tsp. **baking powder**

1 tsp. **baking soda**

¹/₂ tsp. **salt**

¹/₂ cup **chilled butter,
    cut in small pieces**

1 cup **buttermilk**

1 tsp. **vanilla extract**

¹/₂ tsp. **almond extract**

2 **eggs, lightly beaten**

1 **egg white, beaten until frothy**

2 Tb. **granulated sugar**

¹/₂ cup **raspberry preserves or jam**

**Breads**

Preheat oven to 400° F. Mix together flour, ³/₄ cup sugar, baking powder, baking soda and salt. Cut in butter with a pastry blender until mixture resembles coarse meal. In separate bowl, combine buttermilk, vanilla and almond extracts, and the 2 beaten eggs; add to dry ingredients, stirring until moistened. Mixture will be sticky. Turn out on a lightly floured board and knead 4 to 5 times with floured hands. Pat out 8 rounded palm-size circles. Place on a greased cookie sheet. Press a thumb-size indentation on each scone and brush with beaten egg white. Sprinkle with granulated sugar and fill each indentation with raspberry preserves (or jam). Bake for 18 minutes or until golden brown on top. Serve warm. Serves 8.

# MARGAREE SCONES

*Norine Shandro, Bed & Breakfast Inn Margaree
Dawson Creek*

³/₄ cup **milk**

1 **egg**

3 cups **flour**

3 tsp. **baking powder**

¹/₂ tsp. **salt**

1 cup **currants or raisins**

¹/₂ cup **brown sugar**

³/₄ cup **lard**

**white sugar**

Beat together milk and egg, and set aside. Mix flour, baking powder, salt, currants or raisins, and brown sugar in a fairly large bowl. Using your fingers, rub the lard into the flour mixture. When well-blended, add milk and egg. Roll to an inch thickness. Cut with biscuit cutter. Sprinkle scones with white sugar. Bake at 350°F for 20 minutes. Makes about 16.

# BANNOCK

*Fort Nelson Heritage Museum*
*Mile 300 Alaska Highway*

Bannock is a staple food of miners, trappers and other bush travelers in the North. This bannock recipe is a favorite with Fort Nelson residents, who feast on homemade bannock during the community's Heritage Days celebration.

| | |
|---|---|
| 4 cups **flour** | 2 Tb. **baking powder** |
| 2 Tb. **sugar** | 1 tsp. **salt** |
| 3 cups **water** | **raisins (optional)** |

**P**ut all dry ingredients into a bowl and mix. Add water until dough is of dropping consistency. Melt cooking fat in frying pan until hot. Drop tablespoonfuls of mixture into hot fat. Fry until brown all over. Serve with butter and jam. Enjoy! Serves 8 to 10.

# SWEET BEAR CLAW

*Diane Debigare, Rika's Roadhouse & Landing
Mile 275 Richardson-Alaska Highway*

"The best bear claw I've ever tasted," according to one Alaska Highway traveler.

## Dough:
1 cup **butter**
1 Tb. **active dry yeast**
$1/4$ cup **warm water**
3 **egg yolks**
$1/4$ cup **sugar**
$1/2$ tsp. **salt**
$5 1/3$ oz. **evaporated milk**
$3 1/2$ cups **all-purpose flour**

## White Icing:
$9 1/2$ cups **powdered sugar**
1 Tb. **vanilla**
2 tsp. **almond extract**
$1/3$ cup **honey**
1 cup **milk**

## Filling:
$1 1/3$ cups **powdered sugar**
$1/2$ cup **margarine, softened**
$2/3$ cup **white flour**
8 oz. **almond paste**
$3/4$ cup **almond pieces**
$1/4$ cup **raisins**
$1/4$ tsp. **cinnamon**
2 **egg whites**
$1/2$ tsp. **vanilla**
dash **almond extract**

For dough, melt butter in a saucepan. Cool. In a mixing bowl, dissolve yeast in warm water. Stir in egg yolks along with sugar, salt, evaporated milk and cooled butter. Add the flour to the wet ingredients. Beat with mixer on medium speed until well-blended. Dough will be soft and slightly sticky. Refrigerate dough for 1 to 6 hours. Dough may be frozen for future use.

For filling, cream powdered sugar and margarine. Add flour, almond paste, almond pieces, raisins, cinnamon, egg whites, vanilla and almond extract; mix. Cover and refrigerate until firm (1 to 3 hours).

On a very lightly floured surface, roll out refrigerated dough to a 9-inch by 36-inch rectangle (about 1/4 inch thick). Spread filling evenly over the dough, leaving a 1/2-inch strip uncovered at the top long edge of the dough. Starting with the bottom long edge of the rectangle, roll into a log and pinch edge to make a sealed seam. Roll pinched seam underneath and cut log into 12 equal pieces. Make 3 cuts all the way through each piece, about 2/3 of the width of the dough, to form the "toes." Place paws on baking sheets lined with parchment paper, making sure toes fan out to make a claw. Preheat oven to 350°F (or 300°F for a convection oven) while you let claws proof for 15 minutes. Bake for 15 minutes or until lightly browned.

For icing, mix together all ingredients. When claws have cooled, frost with the icing. Serves 12.

# OVERNIGHT COFFEE CAKE

*Linda Cline, Cline's Caswell Lake Bed and Breakfast*
*Mile 88.1 George Parks Highway*

2 cups **flour**
1 tsp. **baking powder**
1 tsp. **baking soda**
1 tsp. **cinnamon**
$1/2$ tsp. **salt**
$2/3$ cup **softened margarine**
1 cup **sugar**
$1/2$ cup **brown sugar**
2 **eggs**
1 cup **buttermilk**

Topping:
$1/2$ cup **brown sugar**
1 tsp. **cinnamon**
1 tsp. **nutmeg**
$1/2$ cup **chopped nuts (optional)**

Combine flour, baking powder, baking soda, cinnamon and salt; set aside. Cream margarine and sugars; add eggs and beat well. Alternate adding dry ingredients and buttermilk to creamed mixture until combined, then spread batter in well-greased 9" x 13" pan. Mix topping ingredients together and spread on top of batter. Cover pan with foil and refrigerate overnight. Bake in preheated 350°F oven for about 45 minutes. Serves 9.

# Soups, Salads & Side Dishes

heep Mountain Lodge is a good example of the lodges that sprang up during the 1940s to serve the growing number of motorists coming to Alaska via the Alaska Highway. Located at Mile 113.5 Glenn Highway, Sheep Mountain Lodge opened in 1946, catering to highway traffic and sportsmen. "Here you may have either rooms or private cabins, relax in the cocktail lounge, or enjoy good meals and Alaskan sociability before the big fireplace," read one of their early advertisements. After 50 years, the lodge still caters to highway traffic, offering "rustic charm and old-fashioned Alaskan hospitality."

# CREST NORTH COAST FISH SOUP

*Chef Wilfred Beaudry, Waterfront Dining Room*
*Crest Hotel, Prince Rupert*

1 litre (approx. 1 qt.) **fish stock**
$^1/_2$ tsp. **each basil, oregano, thyme, salt
  and cracked peppercorns**
4 Tb. **tomato paste**
250 ml (1 cup) **white wine**
250 grams (8.75 oz.) **salmon cubes**
250 grams (8.75 oz.) **snapper cubes**
250 grams (8.75 oz.) **halibut cubes**
8 **prawns**
8 **clams**
$^1/_2$ **Dungeness crab**

Combine all ingredients in a pot and cook covered until clams open. Discard any unopened shells, and divide equally into four large soup bowls. Serves 4.

# HELL'S GATE SALMON CHOWDER

*Debbie McKinney, Hell's Gate Airtram, Hope*

**Fish Stock:**
**fish frames and trimmings**
**1 bay leaf**
**2 carrots, chopped**
**5 stalks celery, chopped**
**1 large onion, diced**
**1 tsp. salt**
**1/2 tsp. pepper**

**Chowder:**
**1 lb. potatoes, cubed**
**1/2 lb. onions, diced**
**3/4 head of celery, chopped fine**
**1 green pepper, diced**

**1 cup butter**
**1³/₄ cups flour**
**2 qts. milk**
**2 qts. fish stock**
**3/4 lb. salmon, minced**
**1 tsp. pepper**
**1 Tb. salt**
**1/2 tsp. season pepper**
**1/4 tsp. garlic powder**
**1 tsp. parsley flakes**
**pinch of thyme**
**pinch of mace**
**pinch of bay leaf powder**

over fish frames and trimmings, bay leaf, carrots, celery stalks, large onion, 1 tsp. salt and 1/2 tsp. pepper with cold water, bring to a boil, simmer 1 hour and strain. Reserve fish stock. Sauté potatoes, 1/2 lb. of onions, 3/4 head of chopped celery and green pepper in butter. Add flour and stir. Add milk slowly. Add stock. Bring to just under a boil. If too thick, add more stock. Next add salmon and simmer. Lastly add seasoning. Serves 8 to 10.

# ALASKAN-STYLE CLAM CHOWDER

*Robert Siter, Gwin's Lodge, Mile 52 Sterling Highway*

6 cups **milk**
1 large **carrot, shredded**
1¹/₂ stalks **celery, finely chopped**
1 large **potato, finely diced**
2 cups **water**
2 slices **bacon, cooked and finely chopped**
1 medium-sized **onion, finely chopped**
¹/₄ Tb. **ground black pepper**
¹/₈ Tb. **salt**
¹/₄ Tb. **clam base**
12 oz. **chopped clams**
¹/₄ cup **butter**
¹/₄ cup **flour**

Pour milk into medium-sized saucepan and place over low heat until scalded. Sauté carrot and celery, cooking until almost tender, then add potatoes and water, and cook until tender. Add chopped bacon. In a separate pan, sauté onion and add to vegetable mixture. Add pepper, salt, clam base and chopped clams. In a separate pan, melt butter. Remove from heat and add flour, stirring with whisk until smooth. Pour butter/flour mixture into scalded milk, stirring constantly until smooth. Stir in vegetable mixture. Continue to heat until thoroughly hot. Serves 4.

# POTATO CORN CHOWDER

*Trapper Creek Inn and General Store, Trapper Creek*

"To make a hardier soup, add 2 cups of diced, cooked chicken."

1/4 lb. **bacon, diced**
1 cup **chopped onion**
1/2 cup **celery**
4 cups **chicken broth**
2 cups **peeled potatoes, cut into 1/2-inch cubes**
1 10-oz. package **frozen corn**
1 tsp. **salt**
1/8 tsp. **ground pepper**
1/2 pint **heavy cream**

Fry bacon in large saucepan over medium heat until bacon is brown, about 3 minutes. Add onion and celery, cook 3 more minutes. Stir in broth and bring to a boil over high heat. Add potatoes, corn, salt and pepper. Cook 5 to 10 minutes until potatoes are tender. Stir in cream and reduce heat to low. Cover and simmer 3 minutes. Serve with oyster crackers. Serves 4 to 6.

# ITALIAN SAUSAGE SOUP

*David Cohen and Diane Schneider*
*Sheep Mountain Lodge, Mile 113.5 Glenn Highway*

1¹/₂ lbs. mild Italian sausage, cut into ¹/₂-inch-thick slices
2 cloves garlic, minced or pressed
2 large onions, chopped
1 large can (about 28 oz.) Italian-seasoned tomatoes,
   reserve liquid
3 cans (about 14¹/₂ oz. each) beef broth
1¹/₂ cups dry red wine OR water
¹/₂ tsp. dry basil
3 Tb. chopped parsley
1 medium green bell pepper, seeded and chopped
2 medium zucchini, cut into ¹/₂-inch-thick slices
3 cups (about 5 oz.) dry bow-tie pasta
grated parmesan cheese

Cook sausage slices in a deep, 5-quart pan over medium-high heat, stirring often, until lightly browned. Lift out sausage with a slotted spoon and set aside. Discard all but 3 Tb. of fat from the pan. Add garlic and onions to pan; cook over medium heat, stirring often, until onions are soft (about 5 minutes).

Cut up tomatoes; add tomatoes and liquid to pan. Add sausage, broth, wine and basil; stir. Bring to a boil, then reduce heat, cover and simmer for 20 minutes. Stir in parsley, bell pepper, zucchini and pasta. Cover and simmer, stirring occasionally, until pasta and zucchini are tender to bite (10 to 15 minutes). Skim and discard fat from soup. Serve with parmesan cheese. Serves 6.

# KACHEMAK CHOWDER

*Jon and Nelda Osgood*
*Tutka Bay Wilderness Lodge, Homer*

¹/₄ cup **cooking oil**
1 cup **chopped onion**
1 cup **chopped celery**
¹/₂ tsp. **garlic salt**
¹/₂ tsp. **dried dill**
2 cups **diced potatoes**
2 cups **sliced carrots**
4 cups **water**
4 cubes **chicken bouillon, or the equivalent**
4 to 6 cups **seafood, precooked or raw, such as chunks of halibut, salmon or cod, minced clams, ground octopus, shrimp or crab in whatever combination you prefer**
2 cups **canned evaporated milk**
1 can **cream-style corn**
**sprigs of fresh dill**
**fish-shaped crackers**

In a 6-quart soup pot, sauté the onion and celery in the oil until soft. Sprinkle with the garlic salt and dill. Add the potatoes and carrots, and sauté for 10 minutes, stirring frequently. Pour in the water, add the bouillon cubes, cover and simmer for 20 minutes, stirring occasionally. When the potatoes and carrots are tender, add the raw seafood and simmer for 2 to 3 minutes. Then add the cooked seafood. When heated through, add the evaporated milk and corn. Heat, taking care to not let it boil again. Garnish servings with sprigs of fresh dill and fish-shaped crackers. Serves 6 to 8.

# MAE'S KITCHEN VEGETABLE BEEF SOUP

### *Mae's Kitchen, Mile 147 Alaska Highway*

At Mae's Kitchen, this soup is served with thick slices of freshly baked, lightly grilled bread.

$1/2$ lb. **ground beef**
1 28-oz. can **whole tomatoes**
1 48-oz. can **tomato juice**
6 cups **water**
1 **medium onion, diced**
3 **cooked potatoes, diced**
3 cups **frozen mixed vegetables**
$1/4$ cup **beef soup base**
$1/2$ tsp. **Watkins Soup Spice
(or sage, onion powder, garlic powder, pepper and other spices to taste)**

**dash of Worcestershire sauce**
**dash of soy sauce**
**salt to taste**
**margarine to taste**
**brown sugar to taste**

**B**rown meat lightly, drain and set aside. In a large pot, mash tomatoes. Bring tomatoes, juice and water to a boil. Add meat and remaining ingredients. Simmer about 1 hour until done. This soup can be frozen in single-portion servings and used as needed. Serves 8 amply.

# GOLD RUSH CABBAGE SOUP

*Elvis Presley, The Northern Beaver Post*
*Mile 649 Alaska Highway*

5 strips **bacon, chopped**
1/4 cup **chopped onions**
4 Tb. **butter OR margarine**
pinch **cayenne pepper**
pinch **curry powder**
1 tsp. **caraway seed**
1 tsp. **salt**
1/2 tsp. **pepper**
1/2 tsp. **parsley**
1/4 cup **flour**
6 cups **chopped cabbage**
6 cups **water**
2 Tb. **chicken base (or more, to taste)**
1 can **evaporated milk**

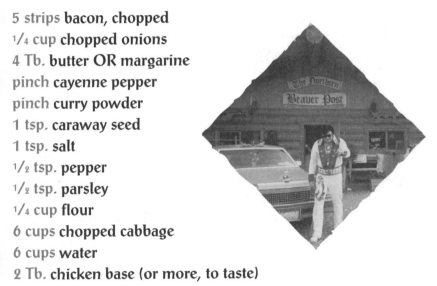

Fry bacon and onions in butter. Add spices, flour and cabbage, and cook for 2 minutes. Add water, chicken base and milk, and cook over low heat until soup thickens. Serves 15 to 20 bowls.

# CABIN COLESLAW

*Joanne Hawkins, Two Choice Cafe, Nenana*

1 small head of cabbage, grated
1 carrot, grated
1 medium-sized onion, diced (optional)
³/₄ cup **Miracle Whip OR mayonnaise**
1 tsp. apple cider vinegar
1 tsp. sugar (more to taste)
1 tsp. yellow mustard
salt, pepper and garlic salt to taste

ix cabbage, carrot and onion. To Miracle Whip add vinegar, sugar, mustard, salt, pepper and garlic salt. Combine dressing with vegetable mixture and toss well. Serves 6.

Joanne Hawkins traveled to Alaska on her own in the winter of 1970, shooting pool and playing her accordion along the way. She arrived in Nenana with $2 in her pocket. Today, she operates 9 businesses in town, including the Bed and Maybe Breakfast and the Tripod Gift Shop. Her secret? "Hard work, a friendly attitude and good service." She still plays the accordion, and the concertina, entertaining up to 1,000 visitors a day in summer. She also planted and maintains the almost 20,000 flowers that blanket Nenana in summer.

# FIDDLEHEAD HOUSE DRESSING

*Deborah Marshall, Fiddlehead Restaurant, Juneau*

"We've been trying for years to describe this adequately, and there seems to be only one description that fits: indescribably good. Originally made by Joan Daniels at the Bread Factory in Anchorage, this salad dressing has been Alaska's favorite for over 20 years."

1/2 cup **good-quality mayonnaise**

1/2 cup **seeded and coarsely chopped tomatoes**

1/3 cup **coarsely chopped onion (1 small)**

2 Tb. **apple cider vinegar**

2 Tb. **safflower oil**

3 to 4 sprigs **fresh parsley, washed and squeezed dry (about 1/2 Tb. freshly chopped parsley)**

Place all ingredients in a large blender or food processor. Purée until smooth. Transfer to a 2-cup container, cover and store refrigerated for up to 3 days. Serve with salad or as a vegetable dip. Yields 1 1/2 cups. (Excerpted with permission from "The Fiddlehead Cookbook.")

# FIDDLEHEAD VINAIGRETTE

*Deborah Marshall, Fiddlehead Restaurant, Juneau*

"This is a classic match for green salads, pasta salads or chilled steamed vegetables."

³/₄ cup **good-quality olive oil**
¹/₄ cup **red wine vinegar**
2 tsp. **Dijon mustard**
¹/₂ tsp. **minced garlic (1 small clove)**
¹/₂ tsp. **salt**
¹/₂ tsp. **pepper**
¹/₄ tsp. **dried thyme**

Whisk all ingredients together in a small bowl or pitcher. Store covered for up to 1 week, whisking thoroughly before each use. Yields 1 cup. (Excerpted with permission from "The Fiddlehead Cookbook.")

# GRILLED CHICKEN SALAD

*The Blues Moose Cafe, Yukon Inn, Whitehorse*

| | |
|---|---|
| 3 cups **mixed greens** | 12 **asparagus spears** |
| **tortilla chips** | **Peanut Sauce** |
| **Honey Lime Dressing** | **(recipe follows)** |
| **(recipe follows)** | ¹/₂ cup **feta cheese** |
| 4 4-oz. **chicken breasts** | |

**D**ivide mixed greens evenly on 4 plates, surrounding each with about 10 tortilla chips. Drizzle greens with Honey Lime Dressing. Grill chicken and asparagus, and place on top of greens. Drizzle with Peanut Sauce. Top with feta cheese. Serves 4.

## Honey Lime Dressing:

| | |
|---|---|
| 1 can **frozen lime concentrate** | 2 Tb. **garlic** |
| ¹/₄ cup **honey mustard sauce** | 1 Tb. **pepper** |
| ¹/₄ cup **honey** | ¹/₂ cup **water** |
| ¹/₄ cup **olive oil** | |

Place all ingredients in blender and blend for 3 minutes.

## Peanut Sauce:

| | |
|---|---|
| 1 cup **peanut butter** | 1 cup **soy sauce** |
| ¹/₂ cup **honey (liquid)** | 1 cup **water** |

Place all ingredients in blender and blend for 2 minutes.

# SEAFOAM SALAD

*Jon and Nelda Osgood*
*Tutka Bay Wilderness Lodge, Homer*

1 6-oz. package **lemon or lime gelatin**
2 cups **boiling water**
1¹/₂ cups **pineapple juice (use the juice drained from the canned pineapple)**
2 to 2¹/₂ cups **canned crushed pineapple**
2 cups **creamy cottage cheese**
2 tsp. **horseradish**
1 cup **mayonnaise (may substitute plain nonfat yogurt for some of the mayonnaise)**
¹/₂ cup **chopped walnuts**
1 cup **chopped pimiento-stuffed green olives, drained**
1 cup **diced celery**
**parsley**

In a medium-sized mixing bowl, dissolve the gelatin in the boiling water. Stir in the pineapple juice. Chill until slightly thickened. With an electric mixer, beat the gelatin until foamy. With a rubber spatula, gently fold in the crushed pineapple, cottage cheese, horseradish, mayonnaise, nuts, olives and celery. Mix well. Pour mixture into a glass serving bowl. Chill until firm (4 to 6 hours). Garnish with several sliced pimiento-stuffed green olives and parsley. Serves 12.

# "SECRET INGREDIENT" FRUIT SALAD

*Christine & Corbett Upton*
*Applesauce Inn B&B, Fairbanks*

"Despite the utter simplicity of this recipe, guests invariably ask me, 'What's the secret ingredient!'"

**4 bananas**
**¹/₂ cantalope**
**1 pint blueberries**
**1 8-oz. carton lemon yogurt**

ice bananas and cantalope in a large bowl. Add blueberries. Fold in lemon yogurt. Makes 4 large servings or 8 small servings.

# SMOKED SALMON CAESAR SALAD

*Deborah Marshall, Fiddlehead Restaurant, Juneau*

The world seems to be divided into those who will eat anchovies and those who will not. This variation of the classic Caesar salad brings them together by using smoked salmon instead of anchovies to create a tasty compromise.

16 cups **torn, fresh mixed greens (romaine,**
  **leaf lettuce, spinach, rocket, escarole, lamb's lettuce**
  **or other fresh greens)**
1/2 lb. **Alaskan smoked salmon (not canned), skin**
  **and bones removed**
4 tsp. **Dijon mustard**
1/2 cup **Fiddlehead Vinaigrette (see page 120)**
2 tsp. **minced fresh garlic (2 large cloves)**
1 cup **garlic-flavored croutons**
1/4 cup **freshly grated parmesan cheese**
16 **marinated artichoke hearts**
8 **tomato slices**
8 **cucumber slices**
16 **black olives**

Chill 8 salad plates. Place greens in a very large salad bowl. Break smoked salmon into small pieces, and sprinkle it over greens. In a small bowl, whisk together mustard, vinaigrette dressing and garlic. Add dressing mixture, croutons

Soups, Salads & Side Dishes

and cheese to salad bowl. Using your hands or salad tongs, toss salad 30 times or until thoroughly mixed. Divide salad onto the chilled plates and garnish each with artichoke hearts, tomato and cucumber slices, and black olives. Serve salad at once. Serves 8. (Excerpted with permission from "The Fiddlehead Cookbook.")

# TROPICAL FRUIT SALAD

*Barbara Winkley, Fernbrook Bed & Breakfast, Anchorage*

Serve this colorful fruit salad in a glass bowl, garnished with a sprig of mint or decorative flowers, such as pansies. If desired, serve with Lime Sauce or Poppy Seed Dressing (recipes follow) on the side.

3 to 4 **pineapple slices**
$^1/_2$ **cantaloupe**
$^1/_2$ **papaya**
2 to 3 **bananas**
1 **apple**
1 **orange, peeled**
1 to 2 **passion fruit**

**D**ice and mix fruit. (Note: Sprinkle pulp of passion fruit with sugar and freeze to preserve for out-of-season use.) Seasonal fruits, such as strawberries or raspberries, may also be added to this salad.

## Lime Sauce:

1 8-oz. package **cream cheese,**      $^1/_4$ cup **lime juice**
   at room temperature       2 Tb. **milk**
$^1/_3$ cup **sugar**

**B**eat cream cheese with electric mixer at low speed until smooth. Mix in sugar, lime juice and milk until combined. Yields approximately 1$^1/_2$ cups.

**Poppy Seed Dressing:**

$1/2$ cup **sugar**

$1^1/2$ tsp. **minced red or white onion**

$1/4$ tsp. **paprika**

$1/4$ cup **cider vinegar**

$1/2$ cup **vegetable oil**

2 Tb. **sesame seeds**

1 Tb. **poppy seeds**

**M**ix sugar, onion, paprika and cider vinegar together. Whisk in oil until well combined. Add sesame and poppy seeds. Store in refrigerator until ready to use.

# PENDLETON POTATOES

*Ronald S. Pendleton, Journeymen's B&B, Homer*

6 or 7 **potatoes, boiled with the jackets on and cooled thoroughly (overnight)**
1 regular-size can **cream of chicken soup**
1/2 soup can **of milk**
1/4 stick **of margarine**
1 cup **sour cream**
4 **green onions, sliced**
11/2 cups **grated cheddar cheese**
**Chicken-in-a-Biscuit crackers**
**melted butter**
**paprika**

Peel and shred potatoes. In a saucepan, heat cream of chicken soup, milk, margarine, sour cream and green onions. Pour 1/3 of this sauce into a 2-qt. casserole dish and add 1/2 of the shredded potatoes. Lightly cover with some of the cheddar cheese. Next, layer another 1/3 of the sauce, the other half of the potatoes and the remaining cheese. Pour the rest of the sauce on top.

Crush some crackers and mix with melted butter. Top potatoes with cracker mixture, and sprinkle lightly with paprika. Bake at 350°F until it bubbles, about 30 minutes.

# Main Dishes

**R**ika's Roadhouse, at Mile 275 Richardson Highway, was built by John Hajdukovich, a pioneer prospector, trapper, hunting guide and entrepreneur. The roadhouse opened in 1906, serving the horse-drawn stage line that connected Valdez and Fairbanks. In 1923, Hajdukovich sold it to Rika Wallen, a Swedish immigrant who had managed the roadhouse for him since 1917. Rika ran the roadhouse into the late 1940s, then lived there until her death in 1969 at the age of 94. Alyeska Pipeline Service Co. bought the roadhouse to house pipeline crews during construction of the trans-Alaska pipeline, and later deeded the property to the Delta Historical Society. The society deeded the land to the state of Alaska for a park. Located on 10 acres along the banks of the Tanana River, the roadhouse and historical buildings were renovated and reopened May 28, 1988, as part of Big Delta State Historical Park.

# ALASKAN-STYLE SALMON-STUFFED HALIBUT

*Robert Siter, Gwin's Lodge, Mile 52 Sterling Highway*

$^1/_4$ cup **chopped onion**
$^1/_4$ cup **chopped celery**
4 Tb. **butter, divided**
$^1/_2$ lb. **cooked salmon, flaked**
$^1/_4$ cup **dry bread crumbs**
1 tsp. **grated lemon peel**
$^1/_2$ tsp. **salt, divided**
**pepper**
1$^1/_2$ lb. **halibut fillet, halved**
$^1/_8$ tsp. **paprika**
1$^1/_2$ Tb. **flour**
$^3/_4$ cup **half and half**
$^1/_4$ cup **white wine**

To prepare stuffing, sauté onion and celery in 2 Tb. butter. Stir in cooked salmon, bread crumbs, lemon peel, $^1/_4$ tsp. salt and dash of pepper. Place half of halibut in a buttered baking dish, sprinkle with paprika and spread salmon stuffing evenly over top. Place the remaining halibut on top of the stuffing. Cover the dish and bake at 425°F for 20 to 25 minutes.

Meanwhile, prepare sauce. Melt 2 Tb. butter in small saucepan and stir in flour, a dash of pepper, a dash of paprika, half and half, and white wine. Stir until thickened.

When halibut is finished cooking, top with white wine sauce and serve. Serves 4.

# GRILLED HALIBUT WITH SUN-DRIED TOMATO SAUCE

*Chef Jon Emanuel, Glacier Bay Country Inn, Gustavus*

"This is great when served with wild rice and fresh asparagus."

4 7-oz. **halibut fillets**
1 **shallot, chopped**
1 oz. **white wine vinegar**
2 oz. **chardonnay**
1 oz. **cream**
1/2 lb. **cold butter chopped into 1-oz. pats**
2 oz. **rehydrated sun-dried tomatoes, chopped**
1/2 oz. **fresh basil, chopped**
**salt and white pepper to taste**

Grill fillets over a medium-high heat on a greased grill until done (about 10 minutes per inch of thickness). Meanwhile, in a small saucepan over medium-high heat, boil shallot and vinegar until liquid is almost gone. Add the wine and reduce again until almost dry. Add cream and reduce by half. Turn heat down to low and briskly whisk in butter, one pat at a time, until all is added. Sauce should be smooth and creamy. Strain sauce and return to pot over low heat. Briskly stir in sun-dried tomatoes until sauce has a nice reddish tint. Stir in basil. Season with salt and white pepper. Keep warm (not hot) until ready to spoon over the halibut. Serves 4.

# HALIBUT MORNAY

*Soldotna Inn and Mykel's Restaurant, Soldotna*

**Crab Stuffing:**
8 oz. crab meat
1 cup bread crumbs
1 Tb. minced shallots
1 tsp. minced roasted garlic
1 Tb. chopped parsley
1/8 tsp. hot sauce
2 egg whites
1/2 cup shredded cheddar cheese

4 8-oz. boneless/skinless halibut fillets
white wine to taste
lemon juice to taste
16 oz. alfredo sauce

Combine all of the crab stuffing ingredients except for half of the cheese in a mixing bowl. Season fillets to taste with your favorite seasonings, white wine and lemon juice. Butterfly halibut fillets and stuff with crab filling. Bake stuffed fillets, covered, at 350°F for approximately 30 minutes. Remove from baking dish. Top with alfredo sauce and remaining cheddar cheese. Glaze under broiler until melted. Serve at once. Serves 4.

# HALIBUT SURPRISE

*Margie M. Smith*
*The Bluff House Bed & Breakfast, Ninilchik*

"Margie's famous recipe for a great holiday brunch or potluck."

2 cups **halibut (or shrimp, crab or salmon)**
2 cups **grated cheddar cheese**
6 oz. **cream cheese, cubed**
$1/2$ cup **chopped green onions**
4 cups **milk**
2 cups **Bisquick baking mix**
8 **eggs**
$11/2$ tsp. **salt**

Grease 9" x 13" pan. Layer halibut, cheeses and onion in pan. In blender combine remaining ingredients, or blend 1 minute with a hand beater. Pour into pan. Bake at 400°F for 35 to 40 minutes, or until knife inserted comes out clean. Cool 5 minutes. Serves 6.

**Main Dishes**

# HAPPY HALIBUT

*Sara Sears, Norlite Campground, Fairbanks*

2 lbs. **halibut**
1/2 lb. **scallops**
1/2 lb. **salad shrimp**
1 cup **Swiss OR mozzarella cheese, shredded**
1 package **Knorr's Hollandaise Sauce Mix**
6 to 8 **pimiento strips**
fresh **parsley**

Place halibut in bottom of a lightly buttered, flat, 2-quart baking dish. Layer scallops, then salad shrimp on top of halibut. Sprinkle fish with cheese. In a separate pan, prepare Knorr's Hollandaise mix according to directions, then pour over layered fish. Arrange pimiento strips on top of dish. Bake in 400°F oven for 25 to 30 minutes or until the halibut tests almost done. (Allow about 1/8 inch of halibut to look uncooked; it will finish cooking before it gets to the table.) Garnish with fresh parsley before serving. Serves 6 to 8. (Excerpted with permission from "Sara's Alaskan Seafood Secrets.")

Anyone who has ever stayed at Norlite Campground in Fairbanks would know Sara, if only by the "Love Sara" signs that appear throughout the campground. It has been said in jest that Sara is her middle name, her full-name being "Love Sara 5 mph." She is author of "Have You Hugged A Tourist Lately!", about her experiences running a campground for 30 years.

# HOMESTEAD HALIBUT

*Jean Somers, Homestead House B&B*
*Mile 135 Sterling Highway*

1/2 cup **butter**
1 **garlic clove, chopped**
1 **large onion, chopped**
1 cup **soy sauce**
1/4 cup **sugar**
2 lbs. **halibut**

In a frying pan, cook garlic and onion in butter. Add soy sauce and sugar, and cook until sugar is dissolved. Place halibut in cake pan and pour sauce over fish. Cook fish on barbecue or bake in 350°F oven for 20 minutes or until halibut flakes when tested with a fork. Serves 6.

# UNFORGETTABLE HALIBUT
## (OR CRAB OR SHRIMP OR TUNA)

*Sara Sears, Norlite Campground, Fairbanks*

"This is one that impressed my mother's bridge group. I serve it with a fruit salad and a soft dinner roll. Talk about easy living!"

4 Tb. **butter**

1/2 cup **chopped onion**

1 1/2 cups **sliced mushrooms**

1 cup **chopped celery**

1 lb. **cooked halibut OR**

   3 cans **crab, shrimp or tuna**

1 cup **mayonnaise**

1 can **cream of mushroom soup**

1 cup **light cream**

3 cups **cooked rice**

1/2 cup **slivered almonds**

1 tsp. **curry powder**

2 tsp. **fresh ground pepper**

2 cups **buttered bread crumbs**

Melt butter in heavy saucepan and sauté onion, mushrooms and celery. In a large bowl, combine halibut (or crab, shrimp or tuna) with mayonnaise, mushroom soup, cream, rice, almonds, curry powder and pepper. Stir in sautéed vegetables and pour mixture into a large buttered casserole, topping with buttered bread crumbs. Bake uncovered at 350°F for 30 to 40 minutes. Serves 12. (Excerpted with permission from "Sara's Alaskan Seafood Secrets.")

# BBQ SALMON

*Sandy Grunow, Sergeant Preston's Lodge, Skagway*

³/₄ cup **brown sugar**
¹/₄ cup **salt**
¹/₄ cup **cooking oil**
¹/₄ cup **vinegar**
**whole salmon**

**M**ix together sugar, salt, cooking oil and vinegar. Open fish down center, preferably not separating skin along back. Spread sauce on fish and allow at least ¹/₂ hour to marinate. Put salmon on tin foil and place in barbecue. Once well heated up, turn barbecue down a little. Cook approximately 1 hour. Serves 6 to 10.

# BROCCOLI SALMON CASSEROLE

*Laurie Coates*
*Almost Home Bed & Breakfast/Cabins, Homer*

"Delicious casserole — especially for those of us who don't particularly care for salmon."

¹/₂ cup **chopped onion**
1 Tb. **butter**
1 8-oz. can **cream of celery soup**
1 4-oz. can **mushrooms, drained**
³/₄ cup **grated parmesan cheese**
¹/₂ tsp. **dill**
¹/₂ tsp. **salt**
¹/₄ tsp. **pepper**
2 Tb. **lemon juice**
10 oz. **broccoli spears, cooked**
³/₄ cup **cooked, flaked salmon**

auté onion in butter until tender. Add soup and mix ingredients together. Add mushrooms, cheese, dill, salt, pepper and lemon juice. Mix well. Toss in broccoli and salmon. Pour in shallow, buttered baking dish. Bake at 350°F for 20 minutes. Serves 4.

# COPPER RIVER SALMON CHILI

*Margy Johnson, Reluctant Fisherman Inn, Cordova*

If Copper River king salmon is unavailable, use whatever salmon you can find.

1¹/₂ cups **dried kidney beans**
¹/₄ cup **olive oil**
¹/₂ tsp. **cayenne pepper**
1 tsp. **ground cumin**
1 tsp. **dried oregano**
2 Tb. **chopped garlic**
¹/₂ cup **diced green pepper**
1 cup **diced celery**

1 cup **diced white onion**
4 cups **canned, diced tomatoes packed in purée**
2 Tb. **chili powder, or to taste**
2 lbs. **Copper River king salmon, skinned and boned**
2 cups **grated cheddar cheese**

oak the dried beans overnight in 8 cups water. Cook soaked beans over medium heat until barely tender. Drain and rinse with cold water. Heat the oil in a skillet. Sauté cayenne, cumin, oregano, garlic, green pepper, celery and onion. Add the tomatoes. In a separate, large pot, mix together 3 cups hot water and chili powder. Add the sautéed mixture and the drained beans. Simmer for 20 minutes. Meanwhile, cut the salmon into ¹/₂-inch cubes. Bring 3 quarts of water to a boil. Place the fish cubes in the water and stir gently for 1 minute. Drain in a strainer and rinse gently with cold water. Remove the chili mixture from the heat and fold in the salmon. Garnish each serving with grated cheese and serve with warmed flour or corn tortillas. Serves 8 to 10.

# SALMON ORIENTAL
*Lillian Banaszak*
*The Chilkat Restaurant and Bakery, Haines*

1¹/₂ cups **soy sauce**
1 cup **olive oil**
¹/₄ cup **red wine**
4 **garlic cloves, crushed**
1 tsp. **black pepper**
3 cups **thinly sliced onion**
2 **sockeye salmon fillets, deboned and cut into 1-inch strips**
3 cups **red and green bell peppers, julienned**

Mix soy sauce, oil, wine, garlic, pepper and onion. Pour marinade over salmon and let sit for at least 4 hours. Grill in olive oil over medium heat until salmon is almost cooked. Then add the peppers and finish cooking. Serve over rice. Serves 6.

**Main Dishes**

# SPICY SALMON PATTIES

*Carol Harmon, Harmony Bed & Breakfast, Seward*

"These patties freeze well, so you can enjoy them all winter long."

³/₄ lb. **poached, flaked salmon**
¹/₂ cup **bread crumbs**
1 Tb. **barbecue sauce**
1 Tb. **mayonnaise**
1 tsp. **cajun spice**
1 **egg**
**salt, pepper and garlic powder to taste**

ix all ingredients with hands until well blended. Shape into 4 patties. Fry in margarine until golden brown on both sides. Serve warm with favorite seafood sauce. Serves 4.

# BAKED GINGER LIME SALMON

*Lisa Wax, Tsaina Lodge, Mile 34.7 Richardson Highway*

"The old-timers who still frequent the lodge prefer a simple salmon preparation that doesn't overpower the natural, delicate flavor of the Copper River salmon."

**4 limes**

**¹/₄ cup brown sugar**

**¹/₄ cup soy sauce**

**¹/₄ cup sesame oil**

**1 Tb. grated fresh ginger**

**4 8-oz. salmon filets**

Zest and juice limes. Add brown sugar, soy sauce, sesame oil and ginger. Mix well. Marinate salmon for 1 hour or overnight. Transfer salmon with marinade to an oven-safe baking pan. Bake at 375°F for 15 to 20 minutes. Serves 4.

# SCAMPI LAKE LOUISE STYLE

*Glen Miles, Lake Louise Lodge, Lake Louise*

"This is our house specialty."

2 Tb. butter
2 Tb. margarine
1 dash cayenne pepper
juice from 1/4 fresh lemon
1 tsp. Worcestershire sauce
1 clove crushed garlic
1 dash salt
1/4 carrot
2 slices onion
1/4 green pepper, seeded and sliced
1/4 red pepper, seeded and sliced

2 broccoli crowns, broken into florets
1/2 stalk celery, chopped
2 cauliflower clusters, broken into florets
2 Tb. white wine
12 Alaskan spotted shrimp (or scallops)
1 Tb. butter
2 slices tomato
2 sprigs parsley
lemon wedges
1 dash paprika

Melt 2 Tb. butter and margarine, and add cayenne, lemon juice, Worcestershire sauce, garlic and salt. Sauté vegetables, except tomatoes, for 5 minutes. Add white wine. Add shrimp, and simmer slowly for 3 to 5 minutes until shrimp are barely done. Add 1 Tb. butter. Put into bowl, and garnish with tomato, parsley and lemon wedges. Sprinkle very lightly with paprika. Serve with baked potato. Serves 2.

# CRAB CAKES

*Karen Eldridge*
*Paxson Lodge, Mile 185.5 Richardson Highway*

8 oz. crab meat, broken into small pieces
20 soda crackers, crushed
2 Tb. mayonnaise
1 tsp. Tabasco sauce
1 Tb. lemon juice
$1/4$ small onion, chopped finely
2 eggs, well beaten
$1/8$ tsp. sage
salt and pepper to taste

In a small bowl, mix all the ingredients. Shape into patties and fry in a small amount of butter until brown on both sides. Drain on paper towel and serve. Makes 4 to 5.

# PEPPER CRAB CAKES

*Chef La Mont Caldwell, Alyeska Resort, Girdwood*

Chef La Mont Caldwell is responsible for creating menus and specials for Alyeska Resort's mountain-top Seven Glaciers Restaurant. These crab cakes are served on a bed of corn purée with a cilantro-lime sauce and garnish.

**16 oz.** fresh or frozen Dungeness crab meat
**1 each** red, yellow and green bell pepper, rinsed and diced (reserve half for garnish)
**1/4 bunch** fresh cilantro (save 4 sprigs for garnish)
**1** lemon, zested
**1/4 cup** mayonnaise
Panko bread crumbs
salt
white pepper
olive oil
Corn Purée (recipe follows)
Cilantro-Lime Sauce (recipe follows)

Squeeze crab meat well to remove all excess liquid. Place in bowl and toss to break up some of the larger pieces. Add half of the diced and rinsed bell peppers. Coarsely chop cilantro and add to bowl. Add lemon zest and mayonnaise. Combine all ingredients. Check consistency: Mixture should have the same texture as tuna salad. If too dry, add more mayonnaise. Bind together with Panko bread crumbs. Form into 8 equal-size balls and roll outside in bread crumbs; form into cakes.

You can make your mixture a day in advance, refrigerate and bread just before cooking.

In sauté pan, heat 1 oz. olive oil, cook crab cakes until golden brown on both sides. Remove from pan. Place on paper towels to absorb excess oil. Place 1¹/₂ oz. warm Corn Purée (recipe follows) in center of each of 4 plates. Arrange crab cakes so that one is flat in center of purée and the other leans against it at a 45° angle. Drizzle with Cilantro Lime Sauce (recipe follows) in a zigzagging method. Garnish with fresh small-diced green, yellow and red bell pepper, and fresh sprig of cilantro. Serves 4.

### Corn Purée:

1 8-oz. can **corn purée**

2 oz. **heavy cream**

2 oz. **water**

**cayenne, chili powder,
paprika, salt, white
pepper to taste**

Place corn, cream and water in a saucepan, bring to a simmer. Add spices to taste. Simmer to oatmeal consistency. Hold until ready to serve.

### Cilantro-Lime Sauce:

6 **limes, zested and juiced**

¹/₄ cup **Chardonnay vinegar**

1 **egg**

¹/₂ cup **olive oil**

1 bunch **chopped cilantro**

Combine lime juice, vinegar and egg in blender. Blend at medium speed while drizzling in olive oil to emulsify. Place in mixing bowl and add fresh chopped cilantro, salt and pepper to taste. Add fresh lime zest.

# ARCTIC DIP

*Sherry Berryman, H & H Lakeview Restaurant*
*Mile 99.5 George Parks Highway*

"We are located on the Parks Highway, and we have some loyal customers in Fairbanks 260 miles away who insist that this sandwich is worth the drive!"

5 to 6 oz. **boneless rump roast, cooked rare and sliced wafer-thin**

1 6-inch **sourdough roll, sliced in half and lightly brushed with melted butter**

3 whole **onion slices, thinly sliced and sautéed in butter**

1 to 2 oz. **Swiss cheese, sliced**

3/4 cup **juice from roast**

3/4 cup **water**

Put the sliced beef in a hot pan and toss gently until thoroughly warm. Place the beef as a layer on one side of the sourdough roll, add sautéed onions and top with Swiss cheese. Warm roast juice and water in a saucepan. Place the sandwich, open-faced, under a broiler until the cheese is bubbly. Put the top on the sandwich and cut diagonally. Serve with au jus. We prefer to add some crispy french fries and some of our creamy coleslaw as side dishes to this meal. Serves 1.

# DAWSON PEAKS BEEF BURRITOS

*Carolyn Allen*

*Dawson Peaks Resort, Mile 797 Alaska Highway*

"Serve with a fresh garden salad and refried beans."

| | |
|---|---|
| 1 lb. **ground beef** | $^1/_2$ tsp. **dried jalapeño pepper** |
| 6 oz. **crushed tomatoes** | 1 cup **salsa** |
| $^1/_4$ tsp. **salt** | 4 to 6 **8-inch flour tortillas** |
| 1 tsp. **chili powder** | grated **Monterey Jack cheese** |
| 1 tsp. **crushed red chili pepper** | **jalapeño peppers** |
| $^1/_4$ tsp. **cayenne pepper** | **chopped fresh tomatoes** |
| 1 Tb. **flour** | **sour cream** |

**B**rown meat and drain. Add crushed tomatoes and stir together with beef. Blend salt, chili powder, red chili pepper, cayenne and flour together in $^1/_4$ cup of cold water to make a paste. Add this paste to the beef mixture along with the diced jalapeño peppers. Cook slowly and stir frequently for 20 to 30 minutes. Fill warmed tortillas with approximately $^1/_2$ cup of the meat mixture and 1 Tb. of salsa. Roll and wrap tortillas, and garnish with Monterey Jack cheese, jalapeño peppers, tomatoes and sour cream. Serves 4.

# CALIFORNIA MEAT CLAW

*Diane Debigare, Rika's Roadhouse & Landing*
*Mile 275 Richardson–Alaska Highway*

## Filling:

1¹/₂ oz. **dried tomato halves, chopped**
    **(approximately 15 halves)**
³/₄ cup **provolone cheese, cut into** ¹/₄-**inch cubes**
³/₄ cup **mozzarella cheese, cut into** ¹/₄-**inch cubes**
1¹/₂ cups **grated parmesan**
3 oz. **pepperoni, cut into** ¹/₄-**inch strips**
¹/₂ cup plus 1 Tb. **sour cream**          ¹/₂ tsp. **salt**
2 Tb. **olive oil**          1¹/₂ Tb. **basil**
1¹/₂ cups **chopped onions**          1¹/₂ Tb. **oregano**
¹/₄ oz. **garlic, minced**          ¹/₄ tsp. **thyme**

## Dough:

3¹/₂ to 4 cups **white flour**          ¹/₂ tsp. **salt**
1 package **active dry yeast**          2 **egg yolks**
1 cup **water**          1 **slightly beaten egg yolk**
¹/₄ cup **margarine**          3 Tb. **cold water**

oak tomatoes in boiling water for 5 minutes, then drain. Add provolone, mozzarella, parmesan, pepperoni and sour cream to tomatoes, and mix. In skillet over medium heat, heat olive oil and sauté onion, garlic and salt. Crush the basil, oregano and thyme as you sprinkle them into the skillet. Add sautéed seasonings to the tomato mixture and mix well. Chill 1 to 3 hours before spreading.

For dough, combine 1½ cups flour and the yeast in a mixing bowl, and set aside. In a saucepan, heat and stir the water, margarine and salt until just warm (110°F to 120°F) and the margarine almost melts. Add this to the flour mixture; then add 2 egg yolks. Beat on low to medium speed for 30 seconds, scraping sides of bowl. Add remaining flour and beat on high speed for 3 minutes to have a moderately stiff dough that is smooth and elastic. Shape into a ball, cover and let rise until double. Punch dough down.

On a very lightly floured surface, roll dough to a 9-inch by 36-inch rectangle (about ¼ inch thick). Spread filling evenly over the dough, leaving a ½-inch strip uncovered at the top long edge of the dough. Starting with the bottom long edge of the rectangle, roll into a log and pinch edge to make a sealed seam (see illustration on page 105). Roll pinched seam underneath and cut log into 12 equal pieces. Make 3 cuts all the way through each piece, about ⅔ of the width of the dough, to form the "toes." Place paws on baking sheets lined with parchment paper, making sure toes fan out to make a claw. Mix together 1 egg yolk and 3 Tb. cold water, and brush over each claw. Preheat oven to 350°F (or to 300°F for a convection oven) while you let claws proof for 15 minutes. Bake for 15 minutes or until lightly browned. Serves 12.

# FAMOUS MILE 649ER BBQ RIBS

*Elvis Presley, The Northern Beaver Post*
*Mile 649 Alaska Highway*

5 to 10 lbs. **ribs (plan on about 1 lb. of ribs per serving)**
¹/₂ cup **brown sugar**
juice and pulp of 6 oranges OR ¹/₄ cup **frozen orange juice**
  **concentrate (do not add water)**
1 cup **ketchup**

| | |
|---|---|
| ¹/₄ tsp. **paprika** | ¹/₂ cup **water** |
| ¹/₄ tsp. **pepper** | 1 Tb. **corn starch** |
| 1 tsp. **curry powder** | 2 Tb. **vinegar** |
| ¹/₄ cup **chopped onions** | 1 Tb. **Worcestershire sauce** |
| 1 Tb. **margarine** | 2 Tb. **soy sauce** |

Boil ribs until meat shrinks from bone. While ribs are boiling, mix together brown sugar, orange juice and pulp (or frozen concentrate), ketchup, paprika, pepper and curry powder for barbecue sauce. Set aside. When ribs are ready, add onions, margarine, water, corn starch, vinegar, Worcestershire sauce and soy sauce, and simmer for 1 to 1¹/₂ hours. Remove ribs from water. Coat completely with barbecue sauce and bake at 350°F until sauce is thick and gooey, about 2 hours.

# HERITAGE HOUSE STEW

*Hudson's Bay 1881 Heritage House Restaurant, Quesnel*

"This is not a fast food. Allow yourself 3 hours of cooking time."

| | |
|---|---|
| 6 to 7 lbs. **chuck steak** | 2 cups **turnips** |
| 2 Tb. **oil** | 2 cups **diced celery** |
| 6 cups **cubed carrots** | 2 cups **chopped onion** |
| 1 Tb. **salt** | 2 cups **tomato sauce** |
| 2 tsp. **pepper** | 1/2 cup **margarine** |
| 1 Tb. **sugar** | 1/2 cup **flour** |

Cut steak into 1-inch cubes. Discard bone, fat, gristle and sinew. In a large, heavy pot, add cooking oil. Brown meat on all sides (no liquid should remain). Cover with water and simmer for 1 1/2 to 2 hours until meat is tender. Add carrots, salt, pepper and sugar, and continue to simmer until carrots are barely cooked. Meanwhile, cook turnips separately and discard water. Add celery, onions, tomato sauce and turnips to the pot.

To prepare the gravy, combine margarine and flour in heavy skillet. Cook over low heat, stirring constantly until mixture is a rich brown color. Add liquid from the stew to form a thick gravy. Return gravy to the stew pot. Mix all ingredients gently. Add water, salt and pepper if required. Let simmer for 5 to 10 minutes before serving. Serve with mashed or boiled potatoes and baking powder biscuits. Serves 15 to 20.

# FILET OF BEEF, THREE TOMATO CRUDITÉ

*Chef La Mont Caldwell, Alyeska Resort, Girdwood*

This beef filet is served on a bed of chard and onion and topped with tomato crudité. You may wish to serve with roasted mashed potatoes and a veal demi sauce drizzled in a zigzag design around the plate.

| | |
|---|---|
| 4 8-oz.beef filets | White Chard/Sweet Onion (recipe follows) |
| salt | Tomato Crudité (recipe follows) |
| black pepper | |

**S**eason beef filets with salt and black pepper. Grill or barbecue. Heat White Chard/Sweet Onion mixture in a sauté pan with 1 oz. olive oil. Place equal portions in center of 4 plates; rest beef filet on top. Cover with 2 oz. Tomato Crudité on each filet. Serves 4.

## White Chard/Sweet Onion:

2 yellow onions
2 bunches white chard (fresh spinach may be substituted)
salt, white pepper

**P**eel and julienne onion, and sauté over low heat in pan with 1 oz. olive oil until onion is translucent and tender. Clean chard, and remove stem and stalk with a paring knife. Add to onion and cook until wilted and tender. Season with salt and white pepper. Remove from pan and cool until ready to serve.

**Three Tomato Crudité:**
1 large, ripe, red tomato
1 large, ripe, yellow tomato
4 to 5 tomatillos (small green) tomatoes
1 red onion, diced small
1 Tb. minced garlic
2 Tb. minced capers (plus 1 Tb. caper juice)
2 lemons, zested and juiced
2 Tb. grated parmesan cheese
chopped fresh basil, thyme
    and oregano to taste
$1/4$ cup olive oil
salt, white pepper

Dice all tomatoes and place in bowl. Add onion, garlic, capers and caper juice. Mix together with lemon zest and juice, cheese and herbs. Add olive oil, and season with salt and white pepper. Do not over mix crudité. Over mixing will destroy the tomatoes. Adjust consistency by adding or decreasing olive oil. It should be a thick, chunky consistency.

The centerpiece of Alyeska Resort is the chateau-style Westin Alyeska Prince Hotel (pictured above), which has 2 restaurants: the Katsura Teppanyaki Japanese steak house and the Pond Cafe. The executive chef for Alyeska Resort is Al Levinsohn.

# PAPRIKA BEEF ROLLS

*Cheryl Dutka, Sportsman Inn*
*Pink Mountain, Alaska Highway*

3 (about 1 lb. each) **round steaks**
**salt**
**pepper**
**paprika**
1/2 lb. **mushrooms, sliced**
**onions, sliced thinly**
**pimiento, chopped**
**stuffed olives, sliced**

**dried bread crumbs**
1/2 cup **melted butter**
1 Tb. **boiling water**
1 **egg**
**flour**
6 **whole mushrooms**
2 **small onions**
1 cup **red wine**

Pound steaks until thin; rub in salt, pepper and paprika to taste. Overlap steaks, making 1 large steak. Spread with layer of mushrooms, onions, pimiento, olives and a light sprinkling of bread crumbs. With whisk, combine butter, boiling water and egg. Immediately dribble mixture over bread crumbs. Roll meat up and tie firmly with string. Flour the outside and brown in butter. Place steak in roaster pan with whole mushrooms and small onions. Sprinkle lightly with salt, pepper and paprika. Add red wine. Bake in 350°F oven for about 2 hours. Serves 6.

# SWISS STEAK

*Lisa Ashby, Copper Center Lodge, Copper Center*

"This dish is absolutely delicious, out-of-this-world, quick and easy to make, budget-effective, appealing to all ages, and it melts in your mouth; steak knives not required."

6 6-oz. **cube steaks**
1 cup **flour**
1 **medium onion, seeded and sliced**
2 **green peppers, sliced**
1/4 lb. **carrots, sliced**
1 No. 303 can **tomato sauce**
2 cloves **garlic, minced**
2 Tb. **parsley flakes**
2 Tb. **Worcestershire sauce**
2 Tb. **lemon juice**

Dredge cube steaks in flour and brown in hot, greased skillet. Place on racks in roasting pan. Layer onions, green peppers and carrots on browned steaks. Combine tomato sauce, garlic, parsley flakes, Worcestershire sauce and lemon juice in a saucepan. Bring to a boil and simmer uncovered for 15 minutes. Pour sauce over meat and vegetables. Cover pan with aluminum foil and bake at 350°F for 1 1/2 hours. Serves 6.

# TRULY TENDER PORK CHOPS

*Jan Thacker, Coldfoot Services and Arctic Acres Inn, Coldfoot*

6 center-cut pork chops
1 egg, beaten
Italian-seasoned bread crumbs
1 large can pear halves and juice

Trim all fat from chops. Tenderize with meat hammer until thin. Dip in beaten egg, and coat with bread crumbs. Brown in butter or margarine until golden brown. Place in a 9" x 13" pan, and pour pear juice around chops. Place pear halves around chops. Cover with foil, and bake at 350°F for 30 to 40 minutes. Serves 6.

# BIRCH BARBECUED CHICKEN

*Susan Humphrey, Mile 18 Haines Highway*

Susan Humphrey's recipe uses her own product, Birch Boy Alaskan Birch Syrup. "The birch boy, Evan Humphrey (pictured below), is also known as the 'yellow-haired sap-sicle sucker,'" writes Susan.

**whole fryer chicken, cleaned and cut in pieces OR**
 **4 boneless, skinless chicken breasts**
**³/₄ cup birch syrup**
**³/₄ cup olive oil**
**1 clove garlic, finely minced**
**1 tsp. cumin**
**1 tsp. onion salt**
**freshly ground black pepper**

After cleaning and drying chicken, mix all other ingredients in a glass or plastic container. Add chicken and mix thoroughly with your hands. (This is messy, but it tenderizes the meat and ensures good contact with the marinade.) Cover container and place in refrigerator. Allow meat to marinate at least 24 hours. Remove chicken from marinade and barbecue over hot coals, with a few twigs of green birch, until golden on the outside and cooked through to center. Serves 4.

# MOOSE CREEK CHICKEN

*Chef George Stone (a.k.a. Chicken George),*
*Kantishna Roadhouse, Denali National Park*

"This recipe was originally known as '40 Below Chicken.'"

## Marinade:
1 qt. **liquid smoke**
1/2 gallon **water**
1/4 cup **crushed garlic**
1/2 cup **brown sugar**
1/4 cup **black pepper, cracked**
48 pieces **of chicken**
2 cups **flour**

## Barbecue sauce:
1/4 cup **salad oil**
1/2 cup **bourbon**
1/2 cup **sherry**
3 dashes **soy sauce**
3 dashes **Worcestershire sauce**
4 cloves **crushed garlic**
1 Tb. **black pepper**
1 cup **brown sugar**
1/2 cup **molasses**
1/2 gallon **catsup**

6 oz. **tomato paste**
2 tsp. **dry mustard**

**Main Dishes**

For marinade, mix together the liquid smoke, water, 1/4 cup garlic, 1/2 cup brown sugar and 1/4 cup pepper. Marinate chicken in marinade sauce no longer than 45 minutes. Remove chicken from marinade and cook in oven for 15 minutes at 325°F. Pull chicken out of oven and dredge in flour. Place back in oven and cook for 15 minutes.

For barbecue sauce, mix together oil, bourbon, sherry, soy sauce, Worcestershire sauce, 4 cloves crushed garlic, 1 Tb. pepper, 1 cup brown sugar, molasses, catsup, tomato paste and mustard.

Pull chicken back out of oven and dip in barbecue sauce, place back in oven for 20 minutes, or until it reaches a temperature of 185°F. Serves 48.

# PEACE COUNTRY CHICKEN

*Charles Kux-Kardos, Alaska Cafe & Dining Room*
*Dawson Creek*

4 boneless chicken breasts
8-oz. black forest ham
4 spinach leaves
4 oz. mushrooms, sliced
flour
vegetable oil
bread crumbs

Eggwash:
1 egg
1 tsp. water
combine with wire whisk

Place chicken between two pieces of plastic wrap and pound to even thickness with a wooden mallet. Place equal portions of ham, spinach and mushrooms in middle of each chicken breast and roll, making certain that the ends are tucked inside. Bread rolled chicken by dipping in eggwash, then flour, back into the eggwash and then into the bread crumbs. (Note that chicken is easier to bread when still slightly frozen.) Brown chicken in frying pan in 1 inch of vegetable oil, or use a clean deep-fryer. Bake at 325°F for 20 minutes. Serve with a Florentine sauce. Serves 4.

The distinctive Alaska Hotel, Cafe & Pub is located "55 paces" from Milepost 0 of the Alaska Highway in Dawson Creek, British Columbia. It is owned and operated by Charles and Heidy Kux-Kardos, who purchased the cafe in 1972 and the hotel in 1989. The hotel building dates from the 1930s and the cafe from the 1950s. Charles and Heidy refurbished both establishments and have concentrated on offering fine dining in the Canadian North.

A lover of old cars, Charles Kux-Kardos still owns the first car he ever bought, a 1929 Plymouth Coupe purchased in 1960 when he was 15 years old. In honor of the Alaska Highway's 50th anniversary in 1992, Kux-Kardos led a group of Rolls-Royce and Bentley motorcars up the Alaska Highway. He completed the "Smooth Cruise," as the Alaska Highway trip was dubbed, driving his own Rolls-Royce, a 1956 Silver Cloud I named Princess Daisy.

# TOMATO-BASIL CHICKEN

*Camp Denali and North Face Lodge, Denali National Park*

"Serve with linguini tossed in garlic-parmesan butter and chopped parsley."

1¹/₃ cup **olive oil**
¹/₂ cup **balsamic vinegar**
1 cup **red wine**
1 tsp. **oregano**
2 Tb. **minced garlic**
1 Tb. plus ¹/₂ tsp. **each salt and pepper, divided**
10 **chicken breasts, skinned and cut in half**
1 cup **onions and/or leeks, chopped**
2 cups **mushrooms, sliced thick**
5 lbs. **canned whole tomatoes,**
  **broken or chopped and drained**
¹/₂ cup **fresh basil, chopped**
¹/₂ cup **fresh parsley, chopped**

Combine 1 cup olive oil, vinegar, ¹/₂ cup of the red wine, oregano, 1 Tb. of the garlic, ¹/₂ tsp. salt and ¹/₂ tsp. pepper. Allow flavors to infuse for several hours. Prepare chicken breasts by laying them closely in baking pans. Pour marinade over them. Cover with foil and store in cool place for at least 3 hours.

Sauté onions and the other 1 Tb. of garlic in the other ¹/₃ cup olive oil. Add mushrooms and sauté until mushrooms sweat. Add tomatoes, basil, parsley, and the remaining 1 Tb. salt, 1 Tb. pepper and ¹/₂ cup red wine. Simmer together just enough to mingle flavors, 10 to 15 minutes. Allow to sit in a cool place at least several hours or overnight.

Preheat oven to 375°F. Before cooking, turn chicken pieces in marinade, then re-cover. Cook chicken, covered, 30 minutes in small pans or 40 minutes in large pans. Heat tomato sauce slowly in 2 separate pots (to keep hot while serving). Serve chicken topped with heaping spoonful of tomato sauce. Serves 10. (This recipe can be multiplied by 4 to serve 40, and by 6 to serve 60.)

# SOUPER EASY CHICKEN ENCHILADAS

*Jan Lawson, Reindeer Mountain Lodge, Cantwell*

2 10¹/₂-oz. cans **cream of chicken soup**
1 pint **sour cream**
1 4-oz. can **diced green chilies**
1 4-oz. can **sliced mushrooms**
1 2¹/₂-oz. can **sliced olives**
2 10-oz. cans **chicken**
2 Tb. **vegetable oil**
12 to 14 **corn tortillas**
1 lb. each **Monterey Jack and cheddar cheese,**
   **grated and combined**

Preheat oven to 350°F. Mix cream of chicken soup, sour cream, green chilies, mushrooms, olives and chicken in bowl and set aside. Heat oil in fry pan. Dip each tortilla into hot oil until softened, drain on paper towel. Spread a thin layer of creamed mixture in bottom of a 9" x 12" pan. Spread creamed mixture down the middle of each tortilla, top with grated cheese, roll and place seam-side-down in pan. Reserve some of the creamed mixture and grated cheese and spread over the top of all tortillas when pan is filled. Bake 25 to 30 minutes. Serve with sliced jalapeños. Serves 6 to 8.

# NORTH POLE COFFEE'S FAMOUS CHILI

*LeOrla Wright & Joy Ford,*
*North Pole Coffee House, North Pole*

4 cans (30 oz. each) vegetarian chili beans
2 cups crushed tomatoes
2 shots espresso
cumin
garlic
seasoning salt
Tabasco
shredded cheese
onions
jalapeño peppers

Pour chili beans, tomatoes and espresso into a slow cooker. Season with cumin, garlic, salt and Tabasco to taste. Let simmer for 3 to 4 hours, stirring occasionally. Serve with shredded cheese, onions and jalapeño peppers. Serves 15 to 20.

# BEEF OR VEGETABLE LASAGNA

*Carol Rhoades, Gracious House Lodge*
*Mile 82 Denali Highway*

2 lbs. hamburger*
1 cup chopped onion
1 cup chopped celery
1 cup chopped green pepper
1 6-oz. can tomato paste
2 15-oz. cans Italian tomatoes
3 15-oz. cans tomato sauce
2 cups canned or fresh mushrooms
1/2 cup red wine
parsley, oregano, minced garlic, black pepper and other
   seasonings you like, to taste
3/4 box (12-oz. size) lasagna noodles, place in pan uncooked
15 oz. low-fat cottage cheese OR ricotta (or both)
1 cup fresh parmesan cheese
2 cups reduced-fat mozzarella cheese
1/2 cup cheddar cheese

   * Hamburger can be replaced with 1 cup each steamed cauliflower,
zucchini, yellow squash, spinach and carrots.

**Main Dishes**

**B**rown hamburger, onions, celery and green pepper. Add tomato paste, tomatoes, tomato sauce, mushrooms, red wine and spices, and cook slowly for 2 hours. When sauce is finished, cover bottom of a 6" x 14" dish with a thin layer of sauce. Place a layer of noodles over sauce, then cottage cheese, parmesan, mozzarella and cheddar cheeses, and sauce. Repeat so there are 2 to 3 layers. Refrigerate overnight. Bake at 400°F for 1 hour. Let cool 30 minutes. Serves 16.

**Desserts**

opper Center Lodge, on the Richardson Highway in Copper Center, had its beginnings as the Holman Hotel, and was known as the Blix Roadhouse during the gold rush days of 1897-98. It was the first lodging place in the Copper River Valley, and was replaced by the Copper Center Lodge in 1932, after the original structure burned down. The historic lodge offers 21 rooms with private or shared baths, and a restaurant serving century-old sourdough starter.

# ALASKA RHUBARB PIE

*Susan and Ken Risse*
*The Blue Goose Bed & Breakfast, Fairbanks*

"This is a dessert, but we always serve it at breakfast. It is our specialty."

## Crust:
1/3 cup **cold lard, cut up**
1 cup **flour (cold)**
2 to 3 Tb. **ice-cold water**

## Filling:
4 cups **rhubarb, cut small**
1 1/4 cups **sugar**
1/3 cup **flour**

## Topping:
1 cup **flour (cold)**
1/2 cup **brown sugar**
1 stick **cold butter, cut up**

To make the crust, mix lard and flour in food processor with steel blade until mixture resembles coarse meal. Add water gradually until mixture just starts to form a ball.

To prepare rhubarb for filling, cut the stalks into 1/4-inch pieces cut lengthwise, which makes for a very tender pie with a nice texture. Mix together the rhubarb, sugar and flour in a bowl until sugar starts to dissolve and coats the rhubarb evenly.

For the topping, mix flour and brown sugar in food processor with steel blade. Add butter pieces and process until crumbly.

Roll crust so it fits in 10-inch pie plate. Add filling and then topping, and bake at 400°F for one hour. The pie is done when the filling just starts to bubble. The center will also rise slightly when done. This settles down after you take it out of the oven and it starts to cool. Serves 8.

# CHOCOLATE DREAM PIE

*Dorothy Rutherford, The Shepherd's Inn*
*Mile 72 Alaska Highway*

1 cup less 2 Tb. **flour**
$^1/_2$ cup **butter, at room temperature**
$2^1/_2$ oz. **finely chopped walnuts**
8 oz. **cream cheese, at room temperature**
$^3/_4$ cup **icing sugar**
$^3/_4$ cup **whipped cream**
6 oz. **instant chocolate pudding mix**
2 cups plus 2 Tb. **milk**
**whipped cream and nuts as desired**

Blend flour and butter with pastry blender; add nuts. Press into a 10-inch pie pan and bake at 325°F until golden brown. Chill.

Blend cheese and icing sugar together; gently fold in the whipped cream. Put into chilled pie crust.

Beat pudding mix and milk until mixture thickens and turns from a dark-chocolate color to a milk-chocolate color. Pour over cheese mixture immediately; chill. Serve with whipped cream and nuts. Serves 10.

# COCONUT CREAM PIE

*Harmke DeBruin, Spirit Lake Wilderness Resort*
*Mile 72.3 Klondike Highway*

1 liter (approx. 1 qt.) **milk**
1 400-ml (12-oz.) can **coconut milk**
²/₃ cup **sugar**
4 **egg yolks**
²/₃ cup **cornstarch**
⁴/₅ cup **coconut crumbs**
**baked pie shell**
**whipped cream**

In a regular pot mix together milk, coconut milk, sugar, egg yolks and cornstarch. Stir over medium heat until it thickens. Add coconut crumbs and stir. Put in pie shell and let it cool down. When it is cold enough, decorate it with whipped cream.

# FLAPPER PIE

*Gay Frocklage, 40 Mile Flats, Iskut*

2 cups **milk**

¹/₄ cup **sugar**

2 Tb. **cornstarch**

2 **egg yolks**

1 tsp. **vanilla**

8- or 9-inch graham cracker OR Oreo Cookie crust
   (save 4 Tb. for topping)

meringue or whipped topping

In a double boiler, or a saucepan over medium heat, mix together milk, sugar and cornstarch. Blend well. Add egg yolk, and cook and stir until thick. Remove from heat and mix in vanilla. Pour into crust and top with meringue or whipped topping. Sprinkle reserved crust crumbs over the top. Serves 8.

# THE LODGE
# RHUBARB CRISP PIE

*M.M. Clay, Sportsman's Kispiox Lodge, Hazelton*

"I make the topping for this pie in ice cream bucket amounts and freeze it to use when needed. The amount in the recipe is probably enough for 8 or more pies."

**Uncooked pastry shell**
**3 to 4 cups diced rhubarb (enough to fill the pie shell)**
**1½ cups sugar**
**4 eggs**
**¼ cup flour**
**¼ tsp. salt**
**¼ to ½ cup heavy cream**

**Topping:**

| | |
|---|---|
| 4 cups **rolled oats** | 3 cups **flour** |
| 3 cups **brown sugar** | 1 lb. **butter or margarine** |

Fill the pastry shell with rhubarb. Mix together sugar, eggs, flour, salt and cream, and pour over rhubarb. Bake at 425°F for 20 minutes. Mix together oats, brown sugar and flour; cut in butter. When rhubarb mixture is finished baking, pour enough of the oat mixture on top of the rhubarb to amply cover. Freeze the remaining topping for future use. Return pie to oven and bake at 350°F for 40 to 50 minutes until brown. Pie should feel solid in the center when gently pressed with fingertips.

# ROSEHIP TORTE

*Carla Pitzel, Hawkins House Bed & Breakfast, Whitehorse*

"This is our signature cake. Many people have asked me for the recipe, so here it is! I traditionally make this cake with rosehip jelly, but any jelly will do. Be careful slicing this cake, it is light as a feather. A final caution: The dough must be made one day in advance.

## Dough:

²/₃ cup **butter**

²/₃ cup **sugar**

¹/₂ cup **flour**

1 **egg**

1 cup **ground hazelnuts OR almonds**

## Filling:

2 cups **whipping cream**

2 Tb. **icing (powdered) sugar**

1 tsp. **vanilla**

**rosehip jelly (see page 214) or jelly or jam of choice**
**marzipan**

Mix butter, sugar, flour, egg and nuts together in a bowl. Turn dough onto flat surface and knead until it makes a nice soft ball. Wrap dough in plastic, and leave it in the refrigerator for one day.

Cut 5 wax paper rounds to fit 10-inch springform pan [or 9-inch cake pan]; butter each wax paper round and place one at the bottom of the baking pan. Divide the dough into 5 equal pieces and for each layer put a mound of dough in the pan, pressing it to the edges to make a thin layer of dough. Bake each layer at 350°F for about 15 minutes. It is overdone if edges become too brown. Repeat this 5 times. Cool each cake layer and don't forget to peel off the wax paper. I once assembled the whole cake and decorated it beautifully, only to realize that I forgot the wax paper on every layer!

Whip cream until stiff. Add icing sugar and vanilla. Spread rose-hip jelly on one side of each of the 5 layers of cake. On first four layers, cover the jelly or jam with equal amounts of whipped cream as you stack each layer. On the last (top) layer, cover the jelly or jam with rolled marzipan and decorate with marzipan figurines and fresh flowers.

# STRAWBERRY RHUBARB PIE

*Diane Debigare, Rika's Roadhouse & Landing*
*Mile 275 Richardson-Alaska Highway*

**Pie crust:**
2 cups **white flour**
¹/₂ tsp. **salt**
²/₃ cup plus 2 Tb. **shortening**
¹/₄ cup **cold water**

**Pie filling:**
1 cup **water**
1 cup **sugar**
3 Tb. plus 2 tsp. **cornstarch**
3 Tb. plus 2 tsp. **strawberry Jello**
4 cups **frozen rhubarb**
4 cups **frozen whole strawberries**

For crust, stir together flour and salt in a small mixing bowl. Cut in shortening until pieces are the size of small peas. Sprinkle the cold water over the flour, mix well until the dough forms a ball. Divide dough in half. On a lightly floured surface, roll each half into a circle. Wrap one half of the pastry around a rolling pin and unroll onto a 10-inch pie plate. Be careful not to stretch the pastry dough.

For pie filling, boil 1 cup water, sugar, cornstarch and Jello for 5

**Desserts**

minutes. You will use 2 cups of this mixture for the pie. Pour 1/3 of the measured filling into the bottom of the pie shell. Add rhubarb, and pour another 1/3 over it. Add strawberries and pour the rest of the Jello mixture over the top. Place the top crust on the pie, trim, seal and crimp edges. Sprinkle top of pie crust lightly with sugar.

Bake at 350°F for approximately 1 hour. Crust should be golden brown. If it browns too fast, cover it with foil.

Convection oven: bake at 340°F for 1 hour, 25 minutes.

The garden behind historic Rika's Roadhouse at Big Delta State Historical Park provides vegetables for the park's Packhouse Restaurant, which serves hearty homemade soups, fresh salads and hefty sandwiches, along with desserts from its own bakery. The sod-roofed museum houses Alaskan artifacts. The roadhouse features historic rooms and a gift shop specializing in items made from Alaskan furs and gold.

# SASKATOON BERRY PIE

*Ramona Holcomb, Purden Lake Resort, Yellowhead Highway*

**Dough:**

2¹/₂ cups **flour**

¹/₄ tsp. **salt**

¹/₂ tsp. **baking powder**

¹/₂ Tb. **brown sugar**

¹/₂ lb. **lard**

¹/₂ cup **cold water**

1 **egg**

1 Tb. **vinegar**

**Filling:**

4 cups **Saskatoon berries, fresh or frozen (if unavailable, substitute any berry, such as blueberries)**

1 cup **sugar**

¹/₄ cup **flour**

2 Tb. **butter**

For the pastry, mix together flour, salt, baking powder and brown sugar, then cut in lard. In a separate bowl, mix together water, egg and vinegar, then add to lard mixture, stirring well. Divide dough in half for top and bottom crusts. Roll out both on floured board. Place bottom crust in pie pan. In a bowl, mix together berries, sugar and flour. Pour mixture into pie pan and dot with butter. Cover top with pastry. Bake at 400°F for 45 minutes or until pastry is browned. Serves 6.

# CHOCOLATE SAUERKRAUT CAKE

*Jan Thacker*
*Coldfoot Services and Arctic Acres Inn, Coldfoot*

²/₃ cup **butter**
1¹/₂ cup **sugar**
3 **eggs, beaten**
¹/₂ tsp. **salt**
¹/₂ cup **cocoa**
2¹/₂ cups **flour**
1 tsp. **baking soda**
1 tsp. **baking powder**
1 cup **cold water**
1¹/₂ tsp. **vanilla**
1¹/₂ cup **sauerkraut (drained and chopped)**

**Frosting:**
3 Tb. **flour**
1 cup **milk**
1 cup **butter**
1 cup **sugar**
1 tsp. **vanilla**

**B**lend butter and sugar until creamy. Add eggs. Sift dry ingredients together. Add dry mixture alternately with the water to the creamed mixture. Stir in and blend the sauerkraut and vanilla. Bake at 350°F for 45 minutes in layer or loaf pans, or 30 minutes in a 9" x 13" pan.

For frosting, cook flour and milk on low heat until thick. Cover and allow to cool. Cream butter and sugar until fluffy. Add to flour-and-milk mixture. Add vanilla and beat until thick and fluffy (about 10 minutes). Spread on cake and sprinkle with nuts, if desired.

# MAYONNAISE CHOCOLATE CAKE

*Dee Hinson, Iron Creek Lodge*
*Mile 596 Alaska Highway*

3 cups **flour**
1 1/2 cups **white sugar**
1/3 cup **cocoa**
2 1/4 tsp. **baking powder**
1 1/2 tsp. **baking soda**
1 1/2 cups **mayonnaise**
1 1/2 cups **water**
1 1/2 tsp. **vanilla**

Sift flour, sugar, cocoa, baking powder and soda together. Stir in mayonnaise, water and vanilla. Stir until well-blended. Bake in 9" x 13" pan for 45 minutes or 2 layer pans for 35 minutes. Top with your favorite frosting or sprinkle with powdered sugar.

# CHOCOLATE POTATO CAKE

*Trisha Costello, The Talkeetna Roadhouse, Talkeetna*

"This is a hearty, moist cake that is even better with hand-whipped cream on top."

³/₄ cup **butter**
2 cups **sugar**
4 **eggs**
³/₄ cup **firmly packed unseasoned mashed potatoes**
³/₄ cup **buttermilk**
3-oz. **baking chocolate, melted**
2 tsp. **vanilla**
³/₄ tsp. **baking soda**
2 cups **flour**
¹/₄ tsp. **salt**
1 cup **nuts (optional)**
**whipped cream (optional)**

Cream butter, and then beat in sugar until light and fluffy. Add eggs, one at a time. Combine potatoes, buttermilk, chocolate and vanilla, and add to butter mixture. Mix all the dry ingredients together and then add to wet mixture. Add the nuts last. Pour into a greased and floured 9" x 13" pan. Bake at 350°F for approximately 50 minutes.

# CRANBERRY CAKE

*Mt. Juneau Inn Bed & Breakfast, Juneau*

1¹/₂ cups **sugar**

2 **eggs**

³/₄ cup **butter, melted and cooled**

¹/₄ cup **almond-flavored syrup**

1¹/₂ cups **flour**

2 cups **frozen cranberries**

¹/₂ cup **chopped pecans**

Preheat oven to 350°F. Grease 9-inch pan (springform pan with removable bottom works well also). Beat sugar and eggs until fluffy. Add melted butter and almond-flavored syrup; mix well. Stir in flour, cranberries and pecans. Pour batter into prepared pan and bake 1 hour.

**Desserts**

# LEMON-ON-LEMON CAKE

*Jon and Nelda Osgood*
*Tutka Bay Wilderness Lodge, Homer*

### Cake:
1 box (3 oz.) **lemon gelatin**
1 box **lemon cake mix**
³/₄ cup **water**
³/₄ cup **vegetable oil**
4 **eggs**

### Glaze:
¹/₃ cup **lemon juice**
2 cups **powdered sugar, unsifted**
2 Tb. **butter, melted**
1 Tb. **water**

Combine gelatin, cake mix, ³/₄ cup water, oil and eggs, and pour into a 9" x 12" baking pan. Bake at 350°F for 30 to 35 minutes. While cake bakes, prepare the glaze. Combine lemon juice, powdered sugar, butter and 1 Tb. water. Remove cake from oven and let cool a little. While it is still warm, punch holes in the cake with a large fork. Pour glaze over. Serves 12 to 16.

Note: Instead of lemon cake mix, you can use yellow or white cake mix, and add 1 Tb. grated lemon peel and 2 tsp. lemon extract.

# MULDROW MUD CAKE

*Camp Denali and North Face Lodge, Denali National Park*

"This rich, moist cake needs only a little frosting."

1¹/₂ cups **strong coffee**
¹/₄ cup **coffee-flavored liqueur**
  **(or other flavored liqueur)**
5 oz. **unsweetened baking chocolate**
1 cup **butter**
2 cups **sugar**
2 cups **unbleached white flour**

1 tsp. **baking soda**
¹/₄ tsp. **salt**
2 **eggs**
1 tsp. **vanilla**
**baking cocoa**
**a chocolate glaze**

Heat coffee and liqueur. Add chocolate and butter, and heat until melted, stirring frequently. When chocolate-coffee mixture is smooth, add sugar and stir until dissolved. Cool until lukewarm.

Sift together flour, baking soda and salt. Gradually add chocolate-coffee mixture, beating well after each addition to avoid lumps in the batter. Add eggs and vanilla. Beat on medium speed for 2 minutes, then turn into a Bundt pan or 10-inch springform pan with center ring that has been greased well and dusted with sifted baking cocoa. Bake at 275°F for about 1¹/₂ hours. When cool, frost with a chocolate glaze.

# WILD BERRY CHEESECAKE

*Deb Kremzar, Bitter Creek Cafe & Mercantile, Stewart*

1/3 cup **margarine**
1 1/4 cups **graham cracker crumbs**
1/4 cup **sugar**
2 lbs. **cream cheese**
2 cans **condensed milk**
4 **eggs**
1/3 cup **flour**
1 Tb. **vanilla**
1/2 tsp. **lemon rind**
1 can **wild berry pie filling**

Preheat oven to 300°F. Melt margarine; add crumbs and sugar. Press crumb mixture onto bottom of a 9- or 10-inch springform pan. Beat cream cheese until fluffy; add condensed milk until smooth. Beat eggs, then add to mixture. Stir in flour, vanilla and lemon rind. Mix well. Bake 1 hour or until done. Top with pie filling. Serves 12.

# BAILEYS CHEESECAKE

*Lisa Wax, Tsaina Lodge, Mile 34.7 Richardson Highway*

"March through May, skiers from around the world gather at Tsaina Lodge, a historic roadhouse, to ski the Chugach Range. While non-skiers opt for traditional desserts, like the strawberry rhubarb pie, the skiers are focused on storing up necessary calories for another day on the mountain. Baileys Cheesecake is often chosen from a long list of decadent desserts. We accompany our cheesecake with a cup of coffee, a wood stove and stories of adventure."

## Crust:
1¹/₂ cups **graham cracker crumbs**
¹/₄ cup **sugar**
¹/₃ cup **melted butter**

## Filling:
1¹/₂ lbs. **cream cheese, softened**
1 cup **sugar**
1 cup **sour cream**
1 tsp. **lemon juice**
1 tsp. **vanilla**
3 eggs **(at room temperature)**
¹/₄ cup **Baileys Irish Creme**

## Topping:
12 oz. **semisweet chocolate chips**
1 cup **whipping cream**

## Garnish:
**strawberries**
**powdered sugar**

Desserts

reheat oven to 350°F. Grease 9-inch springform pan. Combine graham cracker crumbs, sugar and butter. Press into bottom of prepared pan. Bake for 10 minutes, remove from oven and cool. Meanwhile, cream the cream cheese and sugar, then add the sour cream, lemon juice and vanilla, and mix. Add eggs, one at a time, beating after each addition. Slowly mix in Baileys Irish Creme. Pour filling into pie crust and bake for 1 hour or until middle is set. Allow to cool at room temperature, then refrigerate for at least 1 hour before adding topping. For topping, put chocolate chips and whipping cream in a double boiler and heat, stirring constantly, until chocolate chips are melted. Pour over the top of the refrigerated cheesecake. Return cheesecake to refrigerator until chocolate is set. Serve garnished with powdered sugar and fresh strawberries.

**Desserts**

# SOURDOUGH CHOCOLATE CAKE

*Sara Sears, Norlite Campground, Fairbanks*

"This is one of my favorites. It was given to me by an old miner."

$^1/_2$ cup **sourdough starter**
$^1/_4$ cup **powdered milk**
$1^1/_2$ cups **flour**          $1^1/_2$ tsp. **baking soda**
1 cup **warm water**       1 tsp. **vanilla**
1 cup **sugar**            1 tsp. **cinnamon**
$^1/_2$ cup **butter**         2 **eggs**
$^1/_2$ tsp. **salt**          3 oz. **melted, unsweetened chocolate**

Mix together sourdough starter, powdered milk, flour and warm water, and let stand until bubbly (about 2 hours). In a separate bowl, cream together sugar, butter, salt, soda, vanilla and cinnamon, then beat in eggs. Add this mixture and unsweetened chocolate to the starter batter and mix until blended. Bake at 350°F in a greased and floured 9" x 13" pan for about 25 to 30 minutes, or until a toothpick inserted in the center comes out clean. (Excerpted with permission from "Sara's Sourdough Secrets.")

# SAXON SHORT CAKE

*Carla Pitzel, Hawkins House Bed and Breakfast, Whitehorse*

"This recipe is my all-time favorite. It tastes very good, and it is very quick. It is the only 3-ingredient cake I know. It comes from my mother-in-law, Agnes Umbrich, and it is a traditional recipe from her village in Transylvania, Rumania."

For this recipe you will need a deep cake pan with fluted sides that also rims the top of the cake, like a torte. Carla refers to it as a shortcake pan, but these are also called flan pans.

| | |
|---|---|
| 4 eggs, separated | 1 large banana |
| 4 Tb. vanilla sugar* | fresh berries |
| 4 Tb. flour | sweetened whipped cream |

Preheat oven to 400°F. Beat egg whites in a small bowl until stiff, then transfer to a large bowl. Beat egg yolks in a small bowl with sugar until thick and pale yellow in color. Pour yolk mixture over egg whites and mix well; there should be no lumps of meringue. Fold in flour. Spoon into buttered cake pan. Bake in oven at 400°F for 10 minutes, then at 350°F for 20 minutes.

When cake is cooled, remove from pan. Cut a large banana lengthwise into 4 slices. Curve the banana slices along the inside rim on top of the cake. Cover the center of the cake with fresh berries. Top the whole works with sweetened whipped cream.

*Vanilla sugar is found in German specialty stores. If it is not available, use regular sugar and add 1/2 tsp. of vanilla to the beaten egg yolks.

# BEAR PAW COOKIES

*Barbara Jean, Mackintosh Lodge*
*Mile 1022 Alaska Highway*

¹/₂ cup **soft butter or margarine**
1 cup **sugar**
1 **egg**
¹/₂ cup **cocoa**
¹/₄ cup **milk**
1 tsp. **vanilla**
1³/₄ cups **flour**
1 tsp. **baking powder**
¹/₂ tsp. **salt**
1 cup **chocolate chips**
3 **half cashews per cookie**

Cream butter and sugar together. Beat in egg. Stir in cocoa, milk and vanilla. Stir flour, baking powder and salt together and add chocolate chips. Mix well. Drop by spoonfuls onto greased pan. Stick cashews in cookie dough for claw effect. Bake at 375°F for 10 to 12 minutes. Makes 3 dozen.

# BIKER'S ENERGY COOKIES

*Carol Rhoadis, Gracious House Lodge, Mile 82 Denali Highway*

4 cups **oatmeal**
4 cups **flour**
2 tsp. **baking soda**
1 tsp. **salt**
2 cups **margarine**
2 cups **sugar**
2 cups **brown sugar**

4 **eggs**
1¹/₂ cups **peanut butter**
2 tsp. **vanilla extract**
1 cup **milk**
1 cup **powdered sugar**
4 Tb. **milk or more as needed**
2 cups **chocolate chips**

Mix oatmeal, flour, baking soda and salt. Mix margarine, sugar, brown sugar, eggs, peanut butter, vanilla and 1 cup milk in a separate bowl, and then add to dry ingredients. Place in a 16" x 20" pan, and bake at 350°F for 20 to 25 minutes. While baking, combine the powdered sugar and 4 Tb. milk to form a very thin mixture. After removing pan from oven, sprinkle cookies with chocolate chips. As they melt into the warm cookies, add the powdered-sugar-and-milk mixture over the chips. Do not cut into bars until cold. Makes 80 2-inch cookies.

# FANTASY COOKIES

*Deborah Marshall, Fiddlehead Restaurant, Juneau*

"Martha Hopson, a baker with a flair, devised the characteristic flower shape for these cookies that makes them easy to share or savor bite by bite."

1/2 lb. butter (can substitute 1/4 lb. butter and 1/4 lb. margarine but not solely margarine; the butter is important for flavor)

1/2 cup honey

1 1/2 tsp. vanilla extract

1 cup finely ground almonds (to the consistency of coarse meal)

2 1/2 cups sifted unbleached white flour

1/3 cup carob chips OR semisweet chocolate chips

Preheat oven to 350°F and arrange racks so they are evenly spaced in center of oven. In a large mixing bowl, using a wooden spoon or electric mixer set on high, cream together butter and honey until light and fluffy. Beat in vanilla. With a spoon, gently cut almonds and flour into butter and honey mixture using short, straight strokes, as if making pie crust. (Do not beat or knead at this point: The delicate shortbread-like texture of the cookie would be lost.) Just before completely combined, add carob chips. Mix lightly, just until dough comes together in one ball. Do not overmix. Form dough into 1 1/2-inch balls. (An ice cream scoop works well for this purpose.) Place on ungreased cookie sheets. To give cookies the characteristic "Fiddlehead

Fantasy Cookie" shape, flatten each cookie with a rosette-iron form. (Any cookie press, the tines of a fork or the back of a table knife will work just as well.) Bake for 15 minutes, or until lightly golden and slightly puffed in center. Remove cookies from sheets and place on a wire rack to cool. To store, place cooled cookies in an airtight container and keep at room temperature for up to 1 week. Makes 36 cookies. (Excerpted with permission from "The Fiddlehead Cookbook.")

**Desserts**

# OATMEAL COCONUT COOKIES

*Multicultural Heritage Centre, Stony Plain*

Stony Plain's Multicultural Heritage Centre is a repository of historical archives for northern Alberta. The restaurant serves pioneer food.

2 cups **butter or margarine**
3 cups **brown sugar**
2 **eggs**
3 cups **flour**
2 tsp. **baking powder**
1 tsp. **baking soda**
1 tsp. **salt**
3 cups **rolled oats**
1 1/2 cups **coconut**
2 tsp. **vanilla**
**white sugar**

Preheat oven to 350°F. In a mixing bowl, cream together butter and brown sugar. Beat in eggs. In separate bowl, sift together flour, baking powder, baking soda and salt. Add to creamed mixture. Add rolled oats, coconut and vanilla, and combine thoroughly. Shape dough into balls and place on lightly greased cookie sheets. Press balls down with a fork dipped in white sugar. Bake for 10 to 12 minutes, or until lightly browned. Makes approximately 10 dozen cookies.

# THE COOKIE

*Ron Holmstrom, Tiekel River Lodge*
*Mile 56 Richardson Highway*

3 cups **flour**
1¹/₂ tsp. **baking soda**
1¹/₂ tsp. **salt**
1 Tb. **cinnamon**
1 tsp. **baking powder**
3 cups **oatmeal**
1¹/₂ cups **softened margarine**
³/₄ cup **sugar**
1¹/₄ cups **brown sugar, packed**
2¹/₄ tsp. **vanilla**
¹/₄ cup **milk**
2 cups **raisins**
1¹/₂ cups **nuts**
2 cups **chocolate chips**

ift together flour, soda, salt, cinnamon and baking powder. Add oatmeal. In a huge bowl, cream margarine, sugars and vanilla. Add milk. Gradually add flour mixture. Add raisins, nuts and chocolate chips. Form mixture into balls by hand to make 16 to 18 huge cookies. Place on oiled cookie sheets. Bake at 375°F for 19 to 20 minutes.

# LYNELL'S BLUEBERRY BUCKLE

*Sharon Waisanen*
*Spruce Avenue Bed & Breakfast, Kenai Spur Highway*

"Blueberries are abundant in August on the Kenai Peninsula. A favorite picking spot for us is Marathon Road, where we often see caribou."

1 cup **flour**
1¹/₂ cups **quick oatmeal**
1¹/₂ cups **brown sugar**
1 cup **butter**
4 cups **blueberries**
¹/₂ tsp. **cinnamon**

Mix up flour, oatmeal, sugar and butter until crumbly. Spread half of mixture into a 9" x 12" pan. Spread blueberries in pan. Sprinkle with cinnamon and remaining crumb mixture. Bake at 350°F for 30 minutes. (Excerpted with permission from "Spruce Ave. Bed & Breakfast Recipes.")

# RHUBARB STRAWBERRY CRUMBLE

*Carol Oberg, Casey's Bed and Breakfast, Whitehorse*

"Strawberries and rhubarb both grow well here, no matter how cold the winter was. Many other fruits could be substituted with excellent results."

4 cups **chopped rhubarb**

1/2 cup **sliced strawberries**

2 Tb. **lemon juice**

1/4 tsp. **cinnamon**

3/4 cup **sifted flour**

1/8 tsp. **salt**

1/2 cup **brown sugar**

2/3 cup **rolled oats**

1/3 cup **melted butter or margarine**

Arrange fruit in a buttered, 2-quart casserole; sprinkle with lemon juice and cinnamon. Combine dry ingredients, then add melted butter, mix until crumbly and spread over fruit. Bake at 375°F until fruit is tender. Serve with cream or ice cream. Serves 6.

**Desserts**

# PEANUT BRITTLE

*Peter Eden, Alaska Wild Berry Products, Anchorage*

Alaska Wild Berry Products makes thousands of pounds of candy for residents and visitors to Anchorage and Homer. This recipe for peanut brittle yields 17¹/₂ pounds! Readers might want to consider cutting it down to fit their needs.

8 lbs. **sugar**
32 oz. **corn syrup**
1¹/₂ qts. **water**
5¹/₂ lbs. **raw Spanish peanuts**
1¹/₂ sticks **butter**
1¹/₂ Tb. **baking soda**

**M**ix sugar, corn syrup and water together, cooking until temperature reaches 237°F (use candy thermometer). Add peanuts and cook to 300°F. Mix in butter and stir until it melts. Add baking soda and mix well. Pour onto greased and lightly floured baking sheets, stretching to desired thickness. Done when cool to touch. Yields 17¹/₂ lbs.

Alaska Wild Berry Products has been making jam, jellies, sauces and juices from native Alaska berries since 1946. Headquarters is now in Anchorage, where a chocolate waterfall (pictured above) greets visitors to the Alaska Wild Berry Products factory and retail store on International Airport Road. The company introduced their popular chocolate-covered wild berry candies in 1987.

# SOURDOUGH'S GOLDEN BREAD PUDDING

*Jack Lewis, Sourdough Mining Co., Anchorage*

4 cups **diced fresh bread OR** 3¹/₂ cups **diced stale bread
(bread should be measured lightly, not packed)**
3 cups **milk, room temperature**
3 **eggs**
¹/₂ cup **Sourdough Mining Co.'s Hot Buttered Rum Batter**
¹/₄ tsp. **salt**
1 tsp. **vanilla**
¹/₄ cup **drained, crushed pineapple**
¹/₄ cup **raisins**
**juice and grated rind of** ¹/₂ **lemon**
**whipped cream, optional**

Preheat oven to 350°F. Soak bread in milk for 15 minutes. Combine eggs, hot buttered rum batter, salt and vanilla, and beat well. Add pineapple, raisins, and lemon juice and rind. Pour over bread and stir lightly until ingredients are well-blended. Put in baking dish and bake for 45 minutes. Remove from oven when golden brown and brush lightly with additional hot buttered rum batter. Serve warm, with whipped cream if desired.

# FAIRWEATHER SUNSET SORBET (MANGO & STRAWBERRY SWIRL)

*Pastry Chef Lavelle Cozby, Glacier Bay Country Inn, Gustavus*

## Mango:
1/2 cup **water**
1 cup **sugar**
3 cups **puréed mango**
3 Tb. plus 1 tsp. **lime juice**

## Strawberry:
1/2 cup **water**
1 cup **sugar**
3 cups **puréed fresh or frozen strawberries**
3 Tb. plus 1 tsp. **lemon juice**

**fresh mint leaves**

**P**repare mango sorbet first. In a saucepan combine water and sugar, and bring to a boil. Stir until sugar is dissolved. Pour this syrup into a blender or food processor. Add the mango purée and lime juice, and blend until smooth. Strain through a fine strainer into a metal or glass bowl and chill, stirring occasionally to chill evenly. Freeze in an ice cream maker, following manufacturer's instructions. Remove sorbet from cannister and place in bowl in the freezer. Immediately begin the strawberry sorbet. Prepare in the same manner as the mango sorbet, with strawberry and lemon juice in place of mango and lime juice. If using frozen strawberries, there is no need to chill mixture. Freeze in the ice cream maker. When done, spread strawberry sorbet evenly in a large, shallow baking pan. Remove mango sorbet from freezer (it should still be soft), spoon into a pastry bag and, placing the tip of the pastry bag through the strawberry sorbet, pipe straight, even lines of mango sorbet into the strawberry sorbet until all the mango is in the strawberry. Freeze for at least 6 to 8 hours. When ready to serve, scoop sorbet out across the mango and strawberry lines to "swirl" the colors together. Garnish with mint leaves.

# GOOD LITTLE SUCKERS

*Edith Macadam, Cranberry Point B&B*
*Mile 29.9 Klondike Highway*

2 cups **white flour**
$^1/_2$ cup **margarine**
4 tsp. **baking powder**
$^3/_4$ to 1 cup **milk**

**Filling:**
$^1/_2$ cup **margarine**
1 cup **white sugar**
2 Tb. **cinnamon**

**P**ut flour, margarine and baking powder in bowl and cut together with a pastry blender until coarse crumb consistency. Add milk until dough holds together. Roll out dough to a 8" x 12" rectangle. For filling, melt margarine in saucepan, and add sugar and cinnamon. Spread filling on dough. Roll from long side, slice in 1-inch pieces and place on cookie sheet or in muffin pan. Bake 20 minutes at 375°F and enjoy. Freezes well. Makes 1 dozen. Serves 6.

## Sauces, Syrups & Preserves

he old Kantishna Roadhouse served the Kantishna mining camp that was established in 1905 at the confluence of Eureka and Moose creeks, 3 miles northwest of Wonder Lake in what is today Denali National Park and Preserve. Several mining camps appeared almost overnight when gold was discovered in the Kantishna Hills, but most were abandoned a short time later. Kantishna remained, and the new Kantishna Roadhouse—a modern log lodge located near this historic structure—now offers wilderness accommodations for tourists.

# THAI BLACK BEAN SAUCE

*Camp Denali and North Face Lodge, Denali National Park*

Serve this sauce over baked or grilled salmon.

1 cup **dry black beans**
2 Tb. **sesame oil**
2 tsp. **minced fresh ginger**
2 tsp. **minced fresh garlic**
¹/₂ cup **minced red pepper**
¹/₂ cup **minced green pepper**
4 Tb. **honey**

4 Tb. **cider vinegar**
4 Tb. **soy sauce**
12 oz. **unsweetened pineapple juice**
pinch **cayenne pepper**
2 Tb. **cornstarch**
2 Tb. **water**

Soak beans overnight covered in cold water. Drain and cover again in cold water, bring to a boil, simmer for 1¹/₂ to 2 hours. Once beans are tender, strain and run them under cold water. Heat sesame oil in a saucepan over medium heat. Add ginger, garlic, and red and green peppers to oil, and lightly sauté about 3 to 4 minutes, until peppers are slightly soft. Add all the liquid ingredients, cayenne pepper and beans. Bring to boil, then simmer 10 minutes. In a separate dish, mix cornstarch with water. Whisk mixture into the simmering sauce until it thickens. This can be made a day ahead and reheated just before serving. Reheat slowly on a trivet, as it scorches easily. Serves 8.

# LOW-FAT POINT PESTO

*Ila Suchy Dillon, Harmony Point Lodge, Seldovia*

$^1/_4$ cup **walnuts**
$^1/_2$ cup **grated parmesan**
2 Tb. **soy sauce**
4 to 5 cloves **garlic**
1 bunch **spinach, washed and torn**
$^1/_2$ cup **fresh basil**
$^1/_4$ cup **pine nuts**

Combine walnuts, parmesan, soy sauce and garlic in food processor (fitted with metal blade) or blender. Pulse until fine. Add spinach and basil in batches, pulsing lightly between additions and taking care to leave the greens in chunks. Add 1 to 2 Tb. of water if necessary for spreading consistency. Add pine nuts. Serve with pasta or French bread. Serves 8 to 12.

# IRENE'S HAM SAUCE

*Jean Mellish, Nu Houston Motor Inn*
*Yellowhead Highway 16*

²/₃ cup **white sugar**
4 tsp. **dry mustard**
1 cup **white vinegar**
2 **eggs**

Mix sugar and dry mustard together. Add vinegar and mix well. Stir in eggs. Cook all together over medium heat, stirring constantly until thick. Cool and pour into a jar. This will keep for a couple of weeks in the refrigerator. Very good with baked ham.

# APPLE BUTTER

*Trisha Costello, The Talkeetna Roadhouse, Talkeetna*

"This recipe was given to me by my granny. I have used it here at the Roadhouse on numerous occasions with much success."

2 cups **applesauce OR** 4 to 5 **apples**
1 cup **sugar**
1/2 tsp. **cinnamon**
1/4 tsp. **ground cloves**
**sprinkle of salt**

To make your own apple sauce, peel and slice 4 to 5 apples, making sure to remove all core pieces. Cook in a large pot with a lid and just enough water to cover apple pieces. Cook until apples are soft. When cool, mash into sauce.

To make the apple butter, combine the remaining ingredients in a 9" x 13" pan, and bake in a 300°F oven, stirring occasionally, until it is thick enough to spread. It will turn a nice brown color. As it cooks, it will splatter and make a mess—best to foil the racks in your oven. When cool, transfer to jars or plastic container, and store in refrigerator. Use as a spread on peanut butter sandwiches, or as a glaze/side sauce on pork chops or ham.

# CARROT MARMALADE

*Valerie P. Keen, Coachouse Inn, Fort Nelson*

"This is absolutely wonderful, and you can make it year-round at little cost. This recipe can be doubled or tripled."

2 cups **chopped carrot**
1 **lemon or orange (rind and juice)**
3$^1/_2$ **cups white sugar**

ix all of the above ingredients well, and let stand overnight. Boil until fruit is clear. Seal in sterilized jars. Makes 4 cups.

# LOWBUSH CRANBERRY BUTTER

*Jessie Marrs, Alaska's Treehouse Bed & Breakfast, Seward*

1 lb. butter or margarine, softened
$1/2$ cup coarsely chopped raw lowbush cranberries
$1/2$ cup packed brown sugar
$1/4$ cup honey
$1/4$ cup ground walnuts or pecans
$1/2$ cup cranberry sauce
1 Tb. grated orange rind
1 tsp. grated lemon rind

Whip butter at high speed with electric mixer until pale yellow. Add cranberries, brown sugar, honey, walnuts or pecans, cranberry sauce, and orange and lemon rind, and whip until light pink. Butter can be frozen.

# ROSEHIP JELLY

*Carla Pitzel*

*Hawkins House Bed & Breakfast, Whitehorse*

"I love wild rosehips! At Hawkins House we are very busy in the summer, and sometimes I miss the peak seasons for berry picking. If you miss the peak with rosehips, it's okay because they are even better after the first frost. Not only do they become sweeter, but they also become softer and easier to grind. We pick our rosehips right up to the first snowfall in October. Avoid the temptation to use domestic rosehips, they may be bigger, but they may have pesticides and fertilizers."

**rosehips**

**sugar**

1 bottle or 2 packets **liquid pectin**

**R**emove old blooms and stems from the rosehips. Boil 1 cup rosehips with 1¹/₂ cups water until soft. Sieve through a jelly bag. For every 2 cups of extract, add 3 cups of sugar and 1 bottle of liquid pectin. Bring to a boil, and pour into sterilized jars. (If it doesn't set, it becomes rosehip syrup—great on pancakes and waffles!) Makes four 8-oz. glasses using 2 cups extract.

Rosa acicularis, or the prickly wild rose, is a large shrubby plant with large rosy flowers. The rose hip, an orange-red fruit, matures in August and September.

# WALKABOUT TOWN RHUBARB SYRUP

*Sandra Stimson, Walkabout Town B&B, Anchorage*

"This syrup is wonderful on pancakes, waffles and ice cream. I like to can this syrup in 1-pint bottles and give it as gifts. The leftover rhubarb pulp can be frozen and later added to muffins as a tasty, high-fiber ingredient."

6 cups **rhubarb, cut into 1-inch cubes**
6 cups **sugar**
1 Tb. **cinnamon**
$^1/_2$ cup **water (optional)**

Prepare rhubarb by washing it and cutting it into small cubes. Bring sugar, cinnamon and rhubarb to a boil. (Rhubarb usually has a lot of water in it, but you can add the $^1/_2$ cup water if the mixture seems too dry.) Boil mixture for 10 minutes. Cool and strain the syrup. Yields 2$^1/_2$ to 3 cups.

# Contributors

A Fireweed Hideaway Bed and Breakfast
P.O. Box 82057, Fairbanks, AK  99708
(907) 457-2579

A Puffin's Bed and Breakfast Lodge
Box 3, Gustavus, AK  99826
(907) 697-2260 Fax (907) 697-2258

Alaska Cafe & Dining Room
Box 246, Dawson Creek, BC  V1G 3T5
(250) 782-7998 Fax (250) 782-6277

Alaska Sourdough B&B
Box 812, Cooper Landing, AK  99572
(907) 595-1541 Fax (907) 595-1541

Alaska Wild Berry Products
5225 Juneau St., Anchorage, AK 99518
(907) 562-8858

Alaska Wildland Adventures
HC 64 Box 26, Cooper Landing, AK 99572
(907) 595-1279 Fax (907) 595-1428

Alaska's Treehouse Bed & Breakfast
Box 861, Seward, AK  99664
(907) 224-3867 Fax (907) 224-3978

Alaskan Frontier Gardens
P.O. Box 24-1881
Anchorage, AK  99524-1881
(907) 345-6556 Fax (907) 562-2923

Almost Home Bed & Breakfast
1269 Upland Court, Homer, AK  99603
(907) 235-2553 Fax (907) 235-0553

Alyeska Resort
P.O. Box 249, Girdwood, AK  99587
(907) 754-2211 Fax (907) 754-2290

Applesauce Inn Bed & Breakfast
P.O. Box 10355, Fairbanks, AK  99712
(907) 457-3392 Fax (907) 457-3332

Arctic Fox Inn
326 E. 2nd Court, Anchorage, AK  99501
(907) 272-4818 Fax (907) 272-4819

At Schnell's Bed and Breakfast
6608 Chevigny, Anchorage, AK  99502
(907) 243-2074

Bed & Breakfast Inn Margaree
933-111 Ave., Dawson Creek, BC  V1G 2X4
(250) 782-4319

Bed & Breakfast On The Park
602 West 10th Ave., Anchorage, AK  99501
(907) 277-0878

Birch Boy Products
P.O. Box 637, Haines, AK  99827
(907) 767-5660

Birch Grove Inn Bed and Breakfast
P.O. Box 81387, Fairbanks, AK  99708
(907) 479-5781 Fax (907) 479-5781

Birch Haven Inn Bed and Breakfast
233 Fairhill Road, Fairbanks, AK  99712
(907) 457-2451 Fax (907) 457-2452

Bitter Creek Cafe & Mercantile
Box 975, Stewart, BC  V0T 1W0
(250) 636-2166

Blueberry Lodge
9436 N. Douglas Highway
Juneau, AK  99801
(907) 463-5886 Fax (907) 463-5886

The Blue Goose Bed & Breakfast
4466 Dartmouth, Fairbanks, AK  99709
(907) 479-6973 Fax (907) 457-6973

The Blues Moose Cafe, Yukon Inn
4220 4th Avenue, Whitehorse, YT  Y1A 1K1
(403) 667-2527 Fax (403) 668-7643

The Bluff House Bed & Breakfast
P.O. Box 39327, Ninilchik, AK  99639
(907) 567-3605

Brigitte's Bavarian Bed & Breakfast
P.O. Box 2391, Homer, AK  99603
(907) 235-6620

The Cabin Bed & Breakfast
Box 5334, Haines Junction, YT  Y0B 1L0
(403) 634-2626 Fax (403) 634-2626

Casey's Bed and Breakfast
608 Wood Street, Whitehorse, YT  Y1A 2G3
(403) 668-7481

Cedar Creek Vacation Home
P.O. Box 10355, Fairbanks, AK  99712
(907) 457-3392 Fax (907) 457-3332

Cedarvale Cafe
P.O. Box 435, Cedarvale, BC  V0J 2A0
(250) 849-5539

The Chilket Restaurant & Bakery
P.O. Box 691, Haines, AK  99827
(907) 766-2920 Fax (907) 766-2992

Chocolate Drop B&B
P.O. Box 70, Homer, AK  99603
(907) 235-3668 Fax (907) 235-3729

Cinnamon Cache Bakery & Coffee Shop
Box 95, Carcross, YT  Y0B 1B0
(403) 821-4331 Fax (403) 821-4331

Cline's Caswell Lake Bed and Breakfast
HC 89 Box 1601, Willow, AK  99688
(907) 495-1014 Fax (907) 346-2555

Coachouse Inn
Box 27, Fort Nelson, BC  V0C 1R0
(250) 774-3911 Fax (250) 774-3730

Coldfoot Services, Arctic Acres Inn
P.O. Box 9041, Coldfoot, AK  99701
(907) 678-5201 Fax (907) 678-5202

Copper Center Lodge
Drawer J, Copper Center, AK  99573
(907) 822-3245 Fax (907) 822-5035

Cranberry Point B&B
240 N. Klondike Highway, Site 15
Whitehorse, YT  Y1A 5W8

Dawson Peaks Resort
P.O. Box 80, Teslin, YT  Y0A 1B0
(403) 390-2310 Fax (403) 390-2244

Denali National Park Wilderness Centers
Camp Denali and North Face Lodge,
P.O. Box 67, Denali Park, AK  99755
(907) 683-2290 Fax (907) 683-1568

Denali View Bed & Breakfast
HC 89 Box 8360, Talkeetna, AK  99676
(907) 733-2778 Fax (907) 733-2778

Eleanor's Northern Lights B&B
360 State Street
Fairbanks, AK  99701
(907) 452-2598

Fernbrook Bed & Breakfast
8120 Rabbit Creek Road
Anchorage, AK  99516
(907) 345-1954

The Fiddlehead Restaurant
429 W. Willoughby Ave.
Juneau, AK  99801
(907) 586-3150 Fax (907) 586-1042

Finnish Alaskan Bed & Breakfast
P.O. Box 274, Nenana, AK  99760
(907) 832-5628 Fax (907) 832-5656

Fireweed House Bed & Breakfast
8530 North Doublas Highway
Juneau, AK  99801
(907) 586-3885 Fax (907) 586-3385

Fort Nelson Heritage Museum
Alaska Highway, Fort Nelson, BC

40 Mile Flats
Box 35 , Iskut, BC  V0J 1K0

Glacier Bay Country Inn
P.O. Box 5, Gustavus, AK  99826
(907) 697-2288 Fax (907) 697-2289

Gracious House Lodge
Box 88, Cantwell, AK 99729
(907) 822-7307

Gwin's Lodge
HC 64 Box 50, Cooper Landing, AK  99572
(907) 696-4013 Fax (907) 694-4013

H & H Lakeview Restaurant
HC 89 Box 616, Willow, AK  99688
(907) 733-2415 Fax (907) 733-2569

Harmony B&B
P.O. Box 1606, Seward, AK  99664
(907) 224-3661

Harmony Point Lodge
P.O. Box 110, Seldovia, AK  99663
(907) 234-7858 Fax (907) 234-7488

Hatcher Pass Lodge
Box 763, Palmer, AK  97645
(907) 745-5897 Fax (907) 745-1200

Hawkins House Bed and Breakfast
303 Hawkins Street
Whitehorse, YT  Y1A 1X5
(403) 668-7638 Fax (403) 668-7632

Helga's B&B
P.O. Box 1885, Sitka, AK  99835
(907) 747-5497

Hell's Gate Airtram
P.O. Box 129, Hope, BC  V0X 1L0
(250) 867-9277 Fax (250) 867-9279

Heritage House Restaurant
102 Carson Avenue, Quesnel, BC  V2J 1B5
(907) 992-1700

Homestead House B&B
P.O. Box 39490, Ninilchik, AK  99639
(907) 567-3410 Fax (907) 567-3962

Iron Creek Lodge
Mile 596 Alaska Highway, YT  Y0A 1C0
(403) 536-2266

Jan's View Bed & Breakfast
P.O. Box 32254, Juneau, AK  99803
(907) 463-5897 Fax (907) 463-5897

Journeymen's B&B
P.O. Box 3106, Homer, AK  99603
(907) 235-8238

Kantishna Roadhouse
P.O. Box 81870
Fairbanks, AK  99708
(800) 942-7420 Fax (907) 479-2611

Lake House Bed & Breakfast
P.O. Box 1499, Valdez, AK  99686
(907) 835-4752

Lake Louise Lodge
HC01 Box 11716
Glennallen, AK  99588
(907) 822-3311

Lisianski Inlet Lodge
P.O. Box 776, Pelican, AK  99832
(907) 735-2266

Longmere Lake Lodge B&B
P.O. Box 1707, Soldotna, AK  99669
(907) 262-9799 Fax (907) 262-5937

Mackintosh Lodge
Mile 1022 Alaska Highway
Haines Junction, YT  Y1A 3V4
(403) 634-2301 Fax (403) 634-2302

Mae's Kitchen
Mile 147 Alaska Highway
Pink Mountain, BC  V0C 2B0
(250) 772-3215

Manley Roadhouse
Manley Hot Springs, AK 99756
(907) 672-3161

The Northern Beaver Post
P.O. Box 9, Watson Lake, YT Y0A 1C0
(403) 536-2307 Fax (403) 536-7667

Mary's McKinley View Lodge
P.O. Box 13314, Trapper Creek, AK 99683
(907) 733-1555

Nu Houston Motor Inn
P.O. Box 1110, Houston, BC V0J 1Z0
(250) 845-7112 Fax (250) 845-3580

McKinley Foothills B&B
P.O. Box 13089, Trapper Creek, AK 99683
(907) 733-1454 Fax (907) 733-1454

Paxson Lodge
Paxson, AK 99737
(907) 822-3330

Millar Street House Bed & Breakfast
1430 Millar Street, Ketchikan, AK 99901
(907) 225-1258

Purden Lake Resort
P.O. Box 1239, Prince George, BC V2L 4V3
(907) 565-7777

Moose Creek Lodge
Bag 1, Mayo, YT Y0B 1M0

Red Salmon Guest House
P.O. Box 725, Cooper Landing, AK 99572
(907) 595-1733 Fax (907) 595-1533

Morning Glory B&B
1015 Larkspur Ct., Homer, AK 99603
(907) 235-8084

Reindeer Mountain Lodge
P.O. Box 7, Cantwell, AK 99729
(907) 768-2420 Fax (907) 768-2942

Mt. Juneau Inn Bed & Breakfast
1801 Old Glacier Highway
Juneau, AK 99801
(907) 463-5855 Fax (907) 463-5423

Reluctant Fisherman Inn
Box 150, Cordova, AK 99574
(907) 424-3272

Multicultural Heritage Centre
P.O. Box 908
Stony Plain, AB T0E 2G0

Rika's Roadhouse and Landing
P.O. Box 1229, Delta Junction, AK 99737
(907) 895-4938

The Noland House
Box 135, Atlin, BC V0W 1A0
(250) 651-7585 Fax (250) 651-7585

Rock Creek Bed & Breakfast
HC1 Box 3450, Healy, AK 99743
(907) 683-2676

Norlite Campground
1660 Peger Road, Fairbanks, AK 99709
(907) 474-0206 Fax (907) 474-0992

Rose's Forget-Me-Not B&B
502 Monroe Street, Fairbanks, AK 99701
(907) 456-5734 Fax (907) 456-2907

North Country Castle Bed & Breakfast
P.O. Box 111876, Anchorage, AK 99511
(907) 345-7296

Sgt. Preston's Lodge
Box 538, Skagway, AK 99840
(907) 983-252l

North Pole Coffee House
220 Park Way, North Pole, AK 99705
(907) 488-7190 Fax (907) 488-5765

7 Gables Inn
P.O. Box 80488, Fairbanks, AK 99708
(907) 479-0751 Fax (907) 479-2229

Sheep Mountain Lodge
HC 03 Box 8490, Palmer, AK 99645
(907) 745-5121 Fax (907) 745-5120

The Shepherd's Inn
P.O. Box 6425
Fort St. John, BC V1J 4H8
(250) 827-3671

Snowline Bed & Breakfast
11101 Snowline Drive
Anchorage, AK 99516
(907) 346-1631

Soldotna Inn
35041 Kenai Spur Highway
Soldotna, AK 99669
(907) 262-9165

Sourdough Mining Company
5200 Juneau St., Anchorage, AK 99518
(907) 563-2272 Fax (907) 345-8570

Sourdough Paul's Bed and Breakfast
P.O. Box 372, Palmer, AK 99645
(888) 287-7002

Spirit Lake Wilderness Resort
Mile 72.3 Klondike Highway
Carcross, YT Y0B 1B0
(403) 821-4337 Fax (403) 821-4337

Sportsman Inn
Box 88, Pink Mountain, BC V0C 2B0
(250) 772-3220

Sportsman's Kispiox Lodge
Box 2541 RR 1, Hazelton, BC V0J 1Y0
(250) 842-6455 Fax (250) 842-6455

Spruce Avenue Bed & Breakfast
35985 Pioneer Drive, Soldotna, AK 99669
(907) 262-9833 Fax (907) 262-9833

The Talkeetna Roadhouse
P.O. Box 604M, Talkeetna, AK 99676
(907) 733-1351

Tiekel River Lodge
SR Box 110, Valdez, AK 99686
(907) 822-3259

Trapper Creek Inn & General Store
P.O. Box 13209
Trapper Creek, AK 99683
(907) 733-2302 Fax (907) 733-1002

Trapper John's Bed & Breakfast
P.O. Box 243, Talkeetna, AK 99676
(907) 733-2354 Fax (907) 733-2354

Tsaina Lodge
Box 80, Valdez, AK 99686
(907)835-3500 Fax (907)835-5661

Turnagain House
P.O. Box 112916, Anchorage, AK 99511
(907) 653-7500

Tutka Bay Lodge
Box 960, Homer, AK 99603
(907) 235-3905

Two Choice Cafe
Box 419, Nenana, AK 99760
(907) 832-1010 Fax (907) 832-5556

Victorian Heights Bed & Breakfast
P.O. Box 2363, Homer, AK 99603
(907) 235-6357 Fax (907) 235-6357

Walkabout Town B&B
1610 "E" Street, Anchorage, AK 99501
(907) 279-7808 Fax (907) 258-3657

Wintel's Bed & Breakfast
P.O. Box 2812, Kodiak, AK 99615
(907) 486-6935

# Recipe Index